THE END OF THE FRENCH UNITARY STATE?

THE END OF THE FRENCH UNITARY STATE?

TEN YEARS OF REGIONALIZATION IN FRANCE (1982-1992)

edited by

John Loughlin and
Sonia Mazey

FRANK CASS • LONDON

First published in 1995 in Great Britain by
FRANK CASS & CO. LTD
Newbury House, 890-900 Eastern Avenue, Newbury Park, London
IG2 7HH, England

and in United States of America by
FRANK CASS
c/o ISBS
5804 N.E. Hassalo Street
Portland, Oregon 97213-3644

Transferred to Digital Printing 2004

Library of Congress Cataloging-in-Publication Data

A catalogue record for this book is available from the
Library of Congress

This group of studies first appeared in a special issue on 'The End
of the French Unitary State?: Ten Years of Regionalization in
France (1982-1992)' in *Regional Politics & Policy* Vol. 4, No. 3,
published by Frank Cass & Co. Ltd.

Typeset by Frank Cass & Co. Ltd., London

Contents

Introduction

JOHN LOUGHLIN AND SONIA MAZEY

When the French socialists came to power in 1981 for the first time in 23 years, they announced that they would implement a 'vast programme of decentralization' which would be *'la grande affaire du septennat'*. Gaston Defferre, then Minister of the Interior and Decentralization, would take responsibility for these reforms which became known simply as the Defferre Reforms. As part of these reforms, the pre-existing regions (which had the legal status of *établissements publics*) would be strengthened by being upgraded to *collectivités territoriales* (like the departments and munici- palities) and by having democratically elected regional councils. Some island regions, such as Corsica and the overseas territories, were to be given special statutes to take into account their geographical situations.

These reforms had been mooted for some time by the socialists and many of them were contained in the *110 Propositions du Candidat Mitterrand* during the presidentialelection campaign in 1981. They, therefore, came as no surprise. However, what did surprise many commentators was the centrality of their position in the socialists' programme. It had been expected that the socialists would concentrate on traditional left-wing issues such as nationalization and strengthening social welfare provisions. Indeed, in 1945, French left-wing parties had been united in their support for a centralized administrative state, which they regarded as the primary guarantee of democratic equality and essential for effective economic planning. The shift in thinking came during the 1960s, when two shifts occurred. First, several left-wing intellectuals, many of whom were later to join the new Socialist Party founded by François Mitterrand in 1971, became vocal supporters of regional decentralization. A good example of this was Michel Rocard, leader of the PSU (Parti Socialiste Unifié) and later member of the PS, who wrote the provocative book *Décoloniser la Province*. The second important shift was the swing of regionalist groups to the left of the political spectrum. Previously, regionalism in France had been associated with the right and even with authoritarian ideas such as fascism. The ideological shift towards decentralization on the part of the French left was partly a result of their long period in opposition which made it necessary for them to develop an ideology distinct from that of the right. These were the years after May 1968 when it became fashionable to speak of *autogestion* as a method of regulating state-society relationships. However, it was also a response to widespread disillusionment with centralized planning. Growing economic disparities between regions and the impact of international economic recession during the 1970s convinced many on the left of the need to develop regional economic development strategies, based upon a regionalized economic plan. The 1960s and 1970s were also characterized by the revival of regionalist cultural and political movements which found a sympathetic home within the Socialist Party. Indeed, there was often an exchange of personnel between regionalist groups in regions such as Brittany, Corsica, the French Basque Country and Occitania. Meanwhile, economic and industrial disputes began to assume the character of regional protests against a capitalist, centralized state. Inevitably, party political considerations were also involved. Although the left had been out of power at the national level since 1958, local electoral agreements between the Socialist and Communist Parties had produced impressive results. by the late 1970s, many left-wing local councillors – particularly younger ones – were eager for more local autonomy. Thus, the Socialist Party at this time might be described as a broad coalition movement, with traditional centralist Jacobins such as Jean-Pierre Chévènement coexisting alongside regionalists, environmentalists and *autogestionnaires* in favour of greater local democracy, technocrats keen to introduce more effective, regionalized planning, and local political *notables* eager for more power.

Since the 1950s, the regional dimension of French public policy-making, particularly in the area of national planning, had grown by fits and starts. By the late 1970s, consultative regional councils, albeit with limited powers, had already been established. The 'new' regionalization of the planning process by the Socialist Party between 1981 and 1983 was justified by two main arguments. It was intended to serve as an instrument of macro-economic management of the economy. Similarly, abolition of prefectoral *tutelle* and the introduction of directly-elected regional governments were intended to increase local democracy. However, when the party abandoned its neo-Keynesian approach and adopted some neo-liberal approaches in 1983-4, with the appointment of Laurent Fabius as Prime Minister, the meaning of the decentralization reforms changed to take into account this new orientation. Now the primary purpose of decentralization was the modernization of the French state.

After the first socialist defeat in 1986, many socialist policies were either modified or reversed by Jacques Chirac's neo-liberal government. However, the 1982 regional reforms have survived largely intact. To some extent this was because the method chosen by Gaston Defferre to implement the reforms (a 'legislative avalanche') had ensured that they would be irreversible, as Defferre had intended. However, during the period in opposition, the right had come to terms with the new institutions as they provided them with a platform from which they could attack the socialist government. These two factors led to a consensus on the part of all the parties in France with very few exceptions in favour of regionalization and decentralization. The political discourse used to justify the region has, however, undergone a significant change. The primary role of the region is no longer to promote economic redistribution and local democracy. Nor is regionalization any longer (as it was between 1984 and 1986) primarily linked to the modernization of the French state. Instead, regional authorities are now expected to assist private enterprise and regenerate the market economy. Indeed, the privatization of many public services such as transport and housing means that French regional authorities increasingly find themselves in partnership with the private sector. Relationships between regions (and between other local authorities such as departments and municipalities and regions) have thus become increasingly competitive in nature.

In short, the *raison d'être* of French regions has changed since 1982. In part, this development reflects the prevailing neo-liberal, political consensus in France. However, it is also a consequence of European integration. French regions are now competing with each other and with other European regions not only for EU funds, but also for inward investment. Hence the growth of the French regional lobby in Brussels. Thus the logic of regionalization which underpins the 1982 regional reforms has itself undergone an important change.

The papers published in this collection are the revised versions of papers first presented in a conference held at the Erasmus University Rotterdam and the University of Leiden in November 1992. Authors were asked to examine the regional reforms from the perspective of a number of aspects of French public policy and administration. The basic question of the conference was whether French public policy-making had indeed changed under the impact of the reforms and, if so, in what way. What emerges from the collection is that implementation of the 1982 Defferre decentralization reforms has indeed, in certain respects, significantly shifted the territorial distribution of power between Paris and the provinces. A priori administrative and financial control over local governments has been abolished; new policy-making powers and resources have been devolved to the departmental and municipal authorities; and a new tier of regional government has been created. In formal terms, the French state is now in several respects less centralized than at any time since the Revolution.

Yet, formal evaluations of the French 1982 decentralization reforms, though a useful starting point, do not tell the whole story. In particular, they fail to take account of how and why implementation of the reforms has been accompanied by their modification. The past decade has thus been characterized by considerable debate among academics and practitioners alike over the real impact of the 1982 French decentralization reforms. Have French prefects really been deprived of their legendary powers over local councils? How effective, in practice, have local and regional authorities been in promoting distinctive economic and social development strategies? Do local and regional authorities enjoy financial autonomy from the state? And has decentralization prompted the emergence of a new, local political elite?

This volume focuses specifically upon the *regional* impact of the 1982 decentralization reforms. The picture which emerges is a complex one. On the one hand, all contributors agree that, since 1982, French regions have become more powerful financially, politically and economically. Increased financial resources, the introduction of directly elected regional councils and regionalization of the national economic plan has undoubtedly provided new opportunities for regions to assert their political and cultural identity and to promote regional economic development strategies. On the other hand, however, there is also general agreement that hopes (and fears) that the region would become the most influential, sub-national tier of government in France, have yet to materialize. For the moment at least, the political status and policy-making importance of most (but not all) regional authorities remains subordinate to that enjoyed by the long-established, big municipalities and departments. Equally, the administrative influence wielded by Paris ministries over regional policy-making (notably the regionalized planning process) remains considerable. Individual evaluations of the significance of these findings vary: whilst some authors believe the regionalization process has had little significant impact upon centre-periphery linkages within the French politico-administrative system, others are more positive. Significantly, both views acknowledge that some important developments have occurred. The difference perhaps is that whereas for some the pot appears half empty, for others it seems half full. This may also to some extent reflect a difference in basic approaches to social science analysis. One school might be described as *a priori* pessimists and assumes that *any* governmental reforms will fail in any case. Others find a more positive interpretation of the role of government and the possibility of change and see the importance of institutional development in bringing about change. Probably, the truth lies somewhere in between these positions. Institutions do matter, but perhaps not too much while reforms may bring about significant political and societal changes although not always as intended by the reformers. It is clear that real changes have occurred in the French politico-administrative landscape as a result of decentralization and regionalization, but that these changes are not exactly what the reformers of 1981 had in mind.

Evaluating the impact of the 1982 regional reforms is further complicated by the inherent ambiguity of public policy analysis. What criteria are to be used to evaluate the reforms? In fact, there is no simple answer to this question. The content of the reforms themselves provide a logical starting point. Thus, Claude Douence's analysis of the 1982 regional reforms highlights the extent to which they were shaped by the existing regional framework which had been created by earlier regional reforms. As such, the 1982 regional reforms were in certain respects less radical than they might otherwise have been. In particular, as Douence points out, by failing to reduce the number of municipalities (from the legendary figure of 36,000) or to choose between the region and the department, (in order to appease traditional local political *notables*), the reforms actually exacerbated the problem of territorial fragmentation. A related problem raised by Guy Gilbert concerns the failure of the reforms to address the issue of local government finances. Despite sharp increases in regional expenditure levels, the fiscal powers and financial resources of French regions remain extremely limited, especially when compared with those enjoyed by their departmental and municipal counterparts. Other 'missed opportunities' include the limited nature of the response to regionalist pressures, as highlighted by Hintjens, Loughlin and Olivesi's discussion of the impact of the 1982 regional reforms in Corsica and the DOM-TOMs. The reforms also failed to implement promises made to deal with long-standing Breton and French Basque grievances with regard to their regional structures or their linguistic rights. Furthermore, as Patrick Le Galès argues, effective regional economic intervention has been rendered difficult by the failure of the socialist reforms to grant regional authorities specific, economic powers in the first place.

Other contributions seek to explain the discrepancy between the provisions and declared objectives of the reforms on the one hand, and the reality of French regionalization on the other. These studies demonstrate the impact of the wider 'policy environment' upon the working of the reforms. Richard Balme's evaluation of the regionalized planning exercise highlights the extent to which attempts by regional councils to define comprehensive regional plans have been undermined, not only by inadequate resources and inexperience, but also by the continuing importance of national, sectorially defined planning priorities. This problem (of the conflict between territorially defined and sectorially defined policy-making) is further illustrated by Henry Buller and Maryvonne Bodiguel's case-study of regional environmental policy-making. Here also, regional attempts to introduce an integrated policy have been somewhat thwarted by the sectorially segmented nature of the French administration and the reluctance of Paris-based officials to relinquish control over policies and budgets. Patrick Le Galès's analysis of regional economic policy-making similarly reminds us of rivalry between regional and municipal authorities and concludes that many regions are simply unable to compete with the latter in the field of economic policy.

The most striking example of the extent to which implementation of the 1982 regional reform has failed to meet (publicly declared) objectives concerns the supposed reduction in the powers of the regional prefect. As local representatives of the Minister of the Interior, prefects were the traditional embodiment of the power of the centralized Napoleonic state. In an attempt to devolve and democratize this state, the 1982 reforms tried to change this by transferring executive power from the appointed regional and departmental prefects to the elected chairpersons of the regional and departmental councils. *A priori* financial and administrative control over regional decision-making (formerly exercised by the prefect) was also abolished; regional government decisions are now subject only to the *a posteriori* legal and financial control exercised by the administrative tribunals and newly-created regional *Cours des Comptes* which audit local and regional authority budgets. To symbolize these changes, the prefects, in 1982, became *Commissaires de la République*, directly accountable to the Prime Minister. Their new, official role was to coordinate regional economic planning and the activities of the ministerial field services.

In reality, however, 'abolition' of the prefect was extremely short-lived and was, in any case, somewhat illusory. Indeed, in 1987, even their title was officially changed back to prefect. Although the transfer of executive powers from the prefects to the chairpersons of the councils represented a significant reshuffling of administrative powers, the prefect in turn was given responsibility for coordinating all the field services within his territory which, in an important sense, *increased* his powers. However, to some extent the reforms were simply a recognition of already existing situations. In reality, the relations between prefects and local politicians varies across regions, departments and municipalities. Powerful cities and regions such as Paris and Ile-de France or Lyons and Rhône-Alpes whose mayors and regional chairmen were often national politicians, were not dependent on the prefect to provide them with the resources for drawing up and implementing policies. However, underdeveloped rural regions and small municipalities were in this situation. Despite decentralization, the mayors of small towns lacked their own services and continued to rely upon the informal advice of the prefect even after 1982. Often they preferred to do this rather than seek the assistance of the services of the departmental or regional presidents, not least because, as Patrick Le Galès observes, they suspected the latter of political bias. Following pressure from local politicians, legislation introduced in October 1987 transferred responsibility for financial control of budgets of small communes (fewer than 2,000 inhabitants) back to the

Trésorier Payeur Général. The continuing importance of collaboration between prefects and local and regional politicians is clearly reflected in the very small numbers of cases involving local and regional authorities referred to the administrative tribunals and regional *Cours des Comptes* since 1982.

More generally, the 1982 regional reforms have, in several respects, increased the importance of the regional prefect within the politico-administrative system. As Richard Balme, explains, regionalization of the planning process has increased the need for effective territorial coordination of sectoral policies. As head of the ministerial field services, the regional prefect plays a pivotal role in the planning process; it is the regional prefect who prepares the regional plan and who negotiates with the state on behalf of the region during the planning process. Similarly, all applications for European Union structural funds must be prepared by the prefect, on behalf of the state. Moreover, since 1986 successive governments have stressed the need for greater administrative *déconcentration* in order to rationalize and coordinate local authority economic intervention. These concerns were reflected in the 1992 administrative territorial reform, which provided incentives for inter-communal cooperation and further extended the coordinating powers of the prefect in specified sectors. Thus, notwithstanding the formal transfer of regional executive power from the prefect to the elected chairperson back in 1982, prefects retained their importance. Moreover, since 1986 there has been a 'rebalancing' of power in favour of the prefect – and by implication – the centre. Given the inherent tension between political decentralization and effective public policy management, such a development is perhaps not so surprising.

Notwithstanding these limitations, all contributors acknowledge that some important developments have occurred within the French politico-administrative system, which have at least increased the policy-making *capacity* of regions. This has enabled some regions (especially the economically dynamic and politically cohesive ones) to develop a cultural identity and play an important role in the economic policy-making process, albeit one based upon cooperation with the state and/or other local authorities. Moreover, other studies suggest that French regions may yet become more important. Elisabeth Dupoirier's sociological analysis of those regional councillors elected in 1986 suggests that it is possible to identify the emergence of a 'new' regional political elite, which has become increasingly committed to the development of the region. These findings constitute a significant challenge to earlier predictions that the new regional councils would be dominated by traditional local political notables, who would exploit their regional mandate to further municipal and departmental interests. Moreover, as Sonia Mazey points out, European integration has given a further boost to the economic and political importance of French regions. Completion of the European Single Market, the strengthening of the Community's own regional policy, and the European Commission's commitment to the principle of 'subsidiarity' have combined to increase the influence of regional (as well as local) council representatives in the EU policy-making process.

We need also to consider how the 1982 regional reforms fit into the long-term pattern of French regionalization. Since 1958, regional reform has rarely been absent from the French political agenda as successive governments have sought to reform and rationalize the centralized state. As several contributors point out, the Defferre reforms should therefore be viewed as the culmination of a much longer regionalization process initiated by previous right-wing governments. However, while economic and administrative considerations have consistently persuaded governments of the need to reform local government structures, the precise nature of the changes proposed has varied in accordance with the ideological beliefs and political ambitions of those in power. External factors, including financial pressures, economic conditions and European integration have further helped to determine the pace and nature of regionalization. The 1982 French regional reforms, though potentially far-reaching, in many respects represented a continuation and extension of earlier reforms.

Ten years of regionalization and decentralization in France are thus marked by a certain amount of continuity with the past but also by some significant changes. The French politico-administrative system is today much more 'open' than hitherto and, to some extent, more 'chaotic'. It is open in the sense that there now exist new levels of government (for the first time in France there is something approaching local *government* as opposed to simply local *administration*) and new policy actors such as regional and departmental chairpersons not to mention the European level. Furthermore, the traditional sets of relationships between the different actors has changed from the old 'honeycomb' model that existed before 1982 to one that is less easily fitted into a definite pattern. In fact, there exist several different emerging patterns to the extent that even in France, once the uniform state *par excellence*, we may also speak of a *variable geometry* in its formal constitutional structures as well as in the policy capacity across regions and departments. This is why we have described this as 'chaotic', meaning a greater variety than hitherto and an uncertain future both within France and in a European context.

We would like to thank a number of organizations and individuals for making this volume possible. The University Fund of the Erasmus University Rotterdam and the Departments of Public Administration in this university and in the State University of Leiden provided generous financial assistance as did Churchill College, Cambridge. Financial assistance was also provided by the Dutch Ministry of the Interior. Sonja Balsem of the Erasmus University Rotterdam provided expert administrative assistance to the original conference. Special thanks go to Maria Winnubst for both administrative and editorial assistance.

The Evolution of the 1982 Regional Reforms: An Overview

JEAN-CLAUDE DOUENCE

INTRODUCTION

The law of 2 March 1982, concerning the rights and liberties of municipalities, departments and regions, could be considered the starting point of a 'new decentralization' of the entire French administrative system. Nevertheless, it was not the absolute starting point, whether for the regions or the other local authorities. In 1982, the departments and municipalities had been in existence for nearly two centuries. Regions were much more recent, dating from the 1960s and having a weaker legal and political status than the other local authorities, but they too were already playing a significant role in the French local administrative system.

The current regional framework has gradually evolved since the beginning of the Fifth Republic. In 1959-60, a number of decrees divided the French metropolitan territory into 22 regional administrative areas (*circonscriptions d'action régionale*), and most state institutions were gradually reorganized to fit into this new framework (this was particularly true for the administrative services responsible for economic policy and planning). In 1964, the CODER (*Commission de développement économique régional*) was created. This was the first time regions were represented in a public body. One half of its members were chosen from parliament and local councils, the other half from economic and social organizations. A law of 5 July 1972 created regional councils (*établissements publics régionaux*) in each of the regions. As their name illustrates, these were legally and politically less important than the other local authorities which were *collectivités territoriales*. They nevertheless constituted a crucial step in the upgrading of French regions which thereby acquired a kind of hybrid status. These became 'moral persons', that is, legal entities with limited powers which were endowed with financial autonomy and were, to a limited extent, representative of the population. Regions were also created in the four overseas departments (*départements d'outre-mer - DOMs*) in 1972. In 1976, a similar system was adopted for the Ile-de-France region, which had previously been organized as a district.

Did the 'new decentralization' of the 1982 reforms change this pre-existing system? First, the new laws did not bring any geographic modifications to the 26 regions. This was the result of a political decision made by Gaston Defferre and his collaborators who were responsible for drawing up and passing the legislation. They wished to avoid raising the problem of the territorial structure of local communities so as to prevent protracted disputes which might endanger the reforms themselves.

However, the law did transform the nature of the regional councils in three main ways by which the legislators attempted to ensure a break from the past and to make the changes irreversible. These were as follows:

• First, regions would no longer be administratively and financially dependent on the state ('*a priori tutelage*' was replaced by simple '*a posteriori*' supervision).

• Second, executive power was transferred from both the regional and departmental prefects to the elected chairpersons of the departmental and regional councils (the *conseil général* and *conseil régional* respectively).

• Third, regions became fully-fledged local authorities (*collectivités territoriales*) with a corresponding upgrading in their legal and political status. Finally, the strength and legitimacy of the new regional councils was further enhanced by the fact that henceforth they would be elected by universal suffrage.

The 1982 laws were therefore a mixture of continuity and change and created a third level of authority. However, there was little reflection or discussion on the respective roles of the two intermediary levels, the departments and regions, although it was clear that they would be in competition with each other. The tackling of potential problems was deliberately postponed; it was envisaged that further amendments would deal with these difficulties and make the reform eventually more comprehensive (see Article 1 of the 1982 law). Today, ten years on, the existence of regions is no longer in dispute. The role they play in the local administrative system continues to increase, though it remains modest (regional budgets have evolved from under five per cent to about eight per cent of local budgets), although some of the problems that were present at the outset have still not been solved.

On the juridical level, the legislative technique chosen has been rather complex, and, at times, puzzling. The legal texts from 1982 are supposed to modify previous ones although they create entirely different institutions. The result is that we have not one, but several categories of regions accountable to partially different laws. The 20 ordinary regions are regulated by the law of 5 July 1972, modified by the subsequent laws of 2 March 1982, 6 January 1986, and others. The Ile-de-France region follows the regime of the law of 6 May 1976 modified by the same laws. Its statute is very similar to that of the ordinary regions, but with additional powers and resources. This is because its population is 18 per cent of the entire French population. The four overseas regions (Guadeloupe, French Guiana,

Martinique and Réunion) follow the ordinary regime (modified by the law of 5 July 1972), modified by the special laws of 31 December 1982 and 2 August 1984, as allowed by clause 73 of the Constitution. Each overseas region is composed of only one department and has greater powers and resources than its metropolitan counterparts. Corsica's evolution is different: it was initially a region with a special statute (*statut particulier*), but the law of 13 May 1991 turned it into a unique type of local authority. It can no longer be considered a region, either juridically or politically (see further the chapter by Hintjens, Loughlin and Olivesi on the overseas territories in this volume).

As the 1982 laws only provided an outline of the future of the regions and the overall direction of the reforms, there remained many problems to be solved. Two conflicting tendencies developed in subsequent years. On the one hand, the central government and the legislators have tended to minimize the scope of the reforms. On the other, the newly-constituted regional authorities have tried to broaden it and increase their legitimacy and power.

THE CENTRAL GOVERNMENT'S ATTEMPTS TO MINIMIZE THE SCOPE OF THE REGIONAL REFORMS

It seems that the authors of the reforms were concerned about the possible upheavals that might follow them and attempted to contain these within acceptable limits. For instance, the question as to whether the department or the region should be the principal level of government between the municipality and the state was not resolved. After the surprise caused by the launching of the reform, 'departmentalists' (who include President Mitterrand) strongly reasserted their positions. Moreover, as Gaston Defferre had foreseen, the impetus of the reforms tended to diminish with time, leading to a narrowing of their scope. These two factors have militated against the development of the region and have been compounded by the fact that implementation of the regional parts of the decentralization reforms suffered postponements and delays, while the departmental and municipal reforms did not.

The Delays Affecting the Regional Reforms (1982-86)

Article 59 of the law of 2 March stipulated that regions would effectively become fully-fledged *collectivités territoriales* when their councils convened for the first time after direct elections by universal suffrage. However, these elections were continually postponed and did not take place until 16 March 1986. Over a period of four years, therefore, the regions remained *établissements publics* to which the reforms only partially applied. There were a few exceptions where the local political situation made rapid reform indispensable. A law of 2 March granted Corsica its own regional institutions (a *statut particulier* and a regional assembly with more powers than the regional councils of the mainland) and came into effect in August 1982 when the first elections to the Corsican Assembly took place. A law of 31 December 1982 also gave the overseas departments a new form of organization which became effective in early 1983. However, there seemed to be no hurry with regard to the 21 regions of mainland France. The principal reason for this was political: the electoral outlook for the socialists was so poor that the governing party chose to postpone regional elections that they were bound to lose.

It was not until 6 January 1986 that the law governing the organization of the regions was passed. The regional elections took place on 16 March 1986, at the same time as the general elections to parliament. The results showed that the socialists were (from a political point of view) fully justified in their hesitation, since the governing coalition won majorities in just two of the 21 regions. But, from the point of view of giving the new regions a stronger profile, the consequences of the delay in holding the first regional elections were very negative.

During the period of transition, the regions were administered by regional councils whose members were not directly elected but consisted rather of parliamentary deputies and municipal and departmental councillors. Thus, there was no direct link between 'regional' representatives and their constituents. Furthermore, the decentralization laws would be applied to the regional councils only after direct elections were held whereas the newly elected representatives of the municipalities and departments took charge of the decentralization reforms as early as 1982-83.

During this period, the regional authorities elected their own chairpersons, but there was no way executive power could be more democratically legitimate than the body that elected it. Regions received new areas of responsibility yet remained confined within the strict framework of the law (see below). Later, it became very difficult for regions to make up for all the lost time since the laws that were passed subsequently were not really favourable to the regions.

The Limitations on Regional Competencies

From 1972 to 1982, the regions enjoyed limited functions and powers, which were largely a complement to those of the other public authorities. They possessed only consultative powers in relation to national planning and participated in the financing of projects of other public sector institutions. However, direct management was always denied them. The 1982 and 1983 laws significantly increased the prerogatives of the regions in some well-defined sectors; yet the results did not always match expectations and a number of regional competencies eventually proved secondary or marginal (see chapters by Balme and Le Galès in this volume).

The 1982 laws gave local authorities more opportunities to take part in economic decision-making, but they gave the regions the leading role. Only regions could invest in the capital of development companies or regional financing companies. Only regions could grant direct subsidies to companies. In principle, the system was designed so that regions could supervise initiatives at the municipal and departmental levels. Similarly, the reform of national planning policies significantly increased their role in the planning process. Regional authorities had since 1972 been consulted on the regional aspects of national planning, but rather complex procedures had constrained regional interventions at the planning and enforcement stages. The novelty of the 1982 reforms was that regions were henceforth entirely free to adopt their own plans after having consulted the (local) authorities they presided over. They were therefore given general responsibility for economic development and strategic planning, and regional development without any government supervision. The link between national and regional planning policies consisted in the drawing up of a 'planning contract' which was freely negotiated and involved joint decisions and financing. However, the ambitious attempt by Michel Rocard to reinvigorate French planning policy (law of 29 July 1982) soon ran into difficulties, and the planning role of regions has remained marginal. It was too early for the regions to participate effectively in the intermediary plan (law of 7 January 1982). Though planning contracts have not been abolished, they have failed to live up to expectations. In reality, the state has used them to steer the regions towards its own programmes (see chapters by Balme and Le Galès in this volume).

The two 1983 laws transferred a number of responsibilities from the central government to local authorities, which were also given the corresponding financial resources. Regions received their share, but it was much smaller than that of the departments and municipalities. One of the first transfers concerned 'on the job' professional training and apprenticeship. Regions were made entirely responsible for this as a complement to their economic functions. The central government was meant to take part in the decisions only exceptionally. Also, in a rather complex system of shared responsibilities, regions were required to draw up provisional plans concerning secondary schooling as a whole. Within this framework, the departments were given management responsibility for the *collèges* (from 1st to 3rd forms), while the regions received management responsibility for the *lycées* (4th to Upper 6th forms).[1] Other responsibilities transferred to the regions are of more limited interest (for example, subsidies to aquaculture, natural parks and river ports). Professional training should have been the responsibility of the regions, but in fact, in order to fight the economic crisis and increasing unemployment, the state has continued to intervene massively. It currently takes charge of nearly 80 per cent of all public initiatives in this field. The regions, deprived of proper means of action and sufficient budgets, can play only a secondary role. The main problem was that the regions had to take on their new responsibilities with limited financing and staff.

The Limited Resources of the Regions

Before 1982 the regions could not hire their own employees but had to rely on the state. From 1982 onwards, the chaipersons of the regional councils were allowed to recruit their own staff, the only limit being their budgets. However, it was not until 1987 that the statutes of the regional civil service were implemented. Between 1982 and 1987, the regions could only recruit civil servants on secondment from other administrations, or employees on temporary contracts, whereas other local authorities were able to use their existing statutes for their own civil servants. Nevertheless, it was during this period that some regions hired a small number of high-level public managers. They became the core of a 'mission' administration (approximately 5,000 agents out of a total of more than 1,277,000 local civil servants in 1990).

The budgetary resources of the regions had previously been limited due to the small amount of state transfers allocated to regions and the upper limit that was imposed on regional fiscal resources. The abolition of the regional fiscal ceiling was progressive. However, the new planning responsibilities and economic initiatives given to the regions in 1982 were not accompanied by any new financial resources since, legally, they did not constitute transfers of competence. But the state was obliged to transfer the resources necessary to fund other new responsibilities accorded to the regions: a tax on car registrations (*taxe sur les cartes grises*) and specific new grants were therefore transferred to the regions. Unlike the departments and the municipalities, the regions received no DGF (*Dotation Globale de Fonctionnement*). In consequence, the regional share of local authority spending was low (about five per cent) and could not be increased without either raising taxes also levied by other local authorities, or applying to the state for additional resources within the framework of the planning contracts. The whole system was therefore locked in order to control the financial autonomy of the region and the size of their budgets.

The Political Neutralization of the Regional Institutions

This is the area where the law most effectively constrains any attempt by the regions to develop rapidly, compared with other traditional territorial authorities, most notably the departments.

Theoretically, all local authorities are subject to the same regulations and benefit from the same decentralization measures. Each authority freely governs itself through an elected council which, in turn, elects its own executive body (mayors or chairpersons, assisted by deputy-mayors or vice-chairpersons). Legal control is the same for all authorities and is performed by an administrative judge under the supervision of the prefect. Each authority freely organizes its services and exercises its legal competencies.

However, on 10 July 1985, a new electoral law detailing the mode of election of regional councillors was passed. The new system was proportional representation, and the constituencies were none other than the departments. This option may seem surprising, but it was deliberately chosen by the legislators. In 1982, the government had tended to favour proportional representation in a single constituency, namely each region (the system adopted for Corsica and the overseas regions). However, such a solution would have entailed a reform of the electoral system for constitutional reasons. The organic law concerning the senate could only be adopted with the senators' agreement. Thus the constitutional issue would have become a political one. So, in order to avoid holding up the regional reforms, the government chose to compromise. Pierre Joxe, the new Minister of the Interior, declared, during a senate session: 'the department, deeply rooted in ancient cultural and economic history, cannot be neglected'. The choice of the department as the constituency boundary made it possible to set up the new regional institutions without offending the sensibilities of the departmentalists. As a consequence, the basic political and partisan organization of France could remain at the department level, with proportional representation ensuring a dispersion of the political parties. It could be argued that behind this deliberate fragmentation of the electoral process lay the aims of preventing public opinion from developing a 'regional awareness' and precluding the election of coherent majorities in the regional councils.

In the opinion of this author, it is not an exaggeration to interpret these decisions as a kind of venom aimed at half-paralysing the regional institution, all the more so as the municipalities were endowed with a fair and efficient electoral system and the departments were allowed to keep their well-known (if disputable) traditional mode of representation. Moreover, the first regional elections took place on the same day as the parliamentary elections, which reduced their impact. In 1992, the second elections proved this interpretation to be right: only one region had a coherent majority. All the others had to resort to coalitions that were not representative of the electorate, or to fragile 'relative' majorities. Neither the socialist left (which had just one regional chairperson), nor the parliamentary right (19 chairpersons, the Nord-Pas-de-Calais region being headed by an ecologist) complained about the results. The only casualty was the regional institution itself, whose legitimacy and effectiveness have been reduced.

THE ATTEMPT BY THE REGIONS TO ASSERT REGIONAL IDENTITY

The regions have only been able to perform fully for six years, and then in rather difficult conditions. They have nevertheless tried to assert their own identities in the local administrative system. There is a dynamism inherent in all institutions which leads them to assert their existence and justify their functions even beyond the intentions of their creators. This rule also applies to the new regional institutions. Despite the ambiguities and weaknesses of their legal position, they have succeeded in securing a niche in the French administrative system.

The Deep Roots of the Geography of Regional Administration

As indicated above, the geography of French regional administration dates back to 1959-1960. Apart from the Corsican case, this has not been modified since and is not likely to be in the short-term.

Regionalization reforms in France resemble the departmental reforms that took place nearly two centuries earlier. Just like the departments, the regions were created in order to streamline and rationalize the administration of the state (as far as regions were concerned, the problem was the management of the national policy of strategic planning and regional development and the reorganization of the decentralized services of the state). However, like the departments, the regions have also progressively become institutions of local democracy. At the start, their geographical distribution was somewhat artificial, though it was never arbitrary. With time, the regions have established themselves as part of the politico-administrative system of France. It would be very difficult now to reorganize these political and administrative structures by modifying their number and boundaries. (Only the DATAR – *Délégation à l'Aménagement du Territoire et à l'Action Régionale*[2] – can stick to its outmoded techno-cratic vision of regional territories that can be indefinitely redefined according to the objectives of the central government). No attempt to change the regional map over the past thirty years has been strong enough to bring about significant modifications. Public opinion movements which criticized specific aspects of the geographical distribution (for example, historical Brittany, or the Nice region) have never had the political and electoral clout to force political action. The interpretation of this state of affairs is of course ambiguous: on the one hand, the general public is, on the whole, satisfied with the present situation, and, on the other, it is indifferent to an institution it barely knows. Politicians, however, are discreetly but deeply attached to a *status quo* they can easily control. Moreover, the development of administrative structures – whether state services under the responsibility of the regional prefect, or regional services under the responsibility of the chairperson of the regional council – have, in practice, become an irreversible evolution process. Regional bureaucracies have become too powerful for their regional implantation to be seriously questioned.

The parliamentary bill of 6 February 1992 shows how deeply entrenched is the present state of affairs. This law attempted to provide for a form of regrouping and amalgamation of regions in order to reduce their number (the aim was to make regions conform to a mythical 'European template'). The bill was entirely abandoned. All that remains of it is that regions may adopt very flexible cooperation mechanisms. Now, the law even stipulates that the merger of two or more regions can only be performed after formal application by the concerned regional councils and a majority vote in the departmental councils under the authority of the regions. It is hardly likely that any region (let alone the constituent departments) will resort to this cumbersome procedure in the near future, and the chances are that the current distribution into 25 regions (including the overseas regions, but not counting Corsica, which has had its own status since 1991) will remain the same.

The Exercise of the Powers of the Regions

Between 1982 and 1986 the regions began to exercise the new functions granted to them by the law. However, the legislators' aim of allocating the tasks of economic stimulation and coordination was not realized exactly as had been intended. As we have seen, the general planning process has declined and the regions have had to adapt. Nevertheless, they have shown flexibility and have adapted with a certain amount of success. The early regional plans were drawn up hastily, as were the planning contracts they were supposed to inspire. Later, the majority of regions abandoned the idea of drawing up plans and, instead, devoted themselves to the negotiation of contracts with the state. 'Contractualization' has developed considerably, but it has also changed in nature. It is no longer a link between two autonomous planning processes but is rather an experiment in joint planning. This has become a framework for public policies conducted jointly by the state and the region in different fields. The state tries to use planning contracts to steer the regions towards its own projects (the future contracts should be the principal instruments of the national strategic planning policies). However, most of the regions have proved expert and astute enough for the negotiations to be relatively well-balanced and for their programmes to be adopted and partly financed by the state. Political opposition between the (former) left-wing government and the mostly right-wing regions did not hinder the partnership. The perspective should be even better with the election of a new right-wing government in March 1993.

Local economic action, the corollary of planning, has remained modest (see chapter by Le Galès). The regions realized that the system of direct subsidies to enterprises was obsolete as soon as it was launched, and quickly abandoned the policy even before the state changed its economic strategy. In so doing they deprived themselves of a valuable means of action. The adoption of neo-liberal economic policies and the decline of state-controlled economic processes effectively prevented the regions from asserting their pre-eminence over the subordinate authorities they should have controlled. Conversely, they often developed original indirect means to aid economic development. In this field too, the logic of partnership has imposed itself; regions have set up contract-based relations with the local authorities and the other local partners.

The main challenge, and most outstanding success, of regions was the development of a policy for the building and maintenance of school buildings. The regions have found adequate ways of coping with the large increase in the school population: as they were responsible for secondary education, they rapidly built new lycées and improved the functioning of existing ones. Paradoxically, they have shown their management proficiency in a field where the government was initially not ready to trust them. Thanks to a 40 per cent increase in their school budgets over a period of five years (1986-91), the regions managed to offset a serious crisis that the state had allowed to develop. Generally speaking, it can be said that regions have in this sector proved that they are perfectly able to implement consistent and agreed upon public policies in their domain of responsibility. Despite an undeniable lack of legal and financial means, they have proved to be genuine local governments and not mere agents of the central government.

Assertion of the General Role of the Regions

Juridical theory considers that the proper role of *collectivités territoriales* should be the general public interest at the local level. This role gives the local authority a general capacity to act every time a local public interest (that is, a collective need of the population) justifies it. The power is limited by external factors: it must respect freedom of trade and industry and the competencies legally granted to other public entities. This role has been granted to the municipalities and departments for a century.[3] However, there has been considerable debate among constitutional lawyers as to whether regions should be granted a similar general role, or whether, as *établissements publics*, they should only be allowed to exercise specific functions determined by legislation. It is obvious that the problem is not just theoretical, but has serious consequences for the political balance of the local administrative system.

Without any further juridical analysis, our feeling is that juridical theory and administrative practice both imply that regions should be granted this general role. The regions have readily intervened in fields for which the law had granted them no specific authority. They have developed policies in a wide variety of fields: cultural activities, environmental protection, revival of declining rural zones, restructuring of industry and the promotion of international markets. In the cultural field, for instance, the regions at first developed policies to support projects initiated by other organizations, and tended to scatter their subsidies. They subsequently evolved towards a more dynamic and proactive conception of this function, emphasizing a few high-profile actions that were specifically regional such as the funding of regional artists through the FRAC (*Fonds Régional d'Art Contemporain*) or supporting regional drama centres and orchestras. They take an interest in culture, science and technology, and have embarked on the setting up and financing of projects such as environmental museums and multimedia libraries. In short, they have developed original cultural policies to reinforce regional identity. A similar tendency has also emerged with regard to environmental policies (see Bodiguel and Buller in this volume). Global policies have gradually been concretized into specific programmes, for example, the setting up of regional natural parks and the protection of natural environments, or as responses to specific environmental problems such as the management of industrial refuse.

What is important is that the regions have set up a considerable number of public projects based on their own conception of what constitutes the regional interest. Furthermore, the central government has urged them to do so, not out of principle, but out of financial necessity. The recent *Université 2000* project is an exemplary illustration of this trend. The state and all the regions have worked together to define a university development programme, although this is normally the sole prerogative of central government. The regions obviously have a direct interest in the development of universities on their territory and so they have agreed to fund those parts of the programme that interest them. It must also be noted that the regions have developed foreign relations that far exceed what had been envisaged by the legislators who only legitimated transfrontier relations. Some regions have opened up offices to lobby the EU in Brussels, and others have signed cooperation agreements with local authorities in other countries such as the *Communauté de Travail des Pyrénées* (see chapter by Mazey in this volume). A law passed in 1992 merely acknowledges what has been termed the 'spontaneous evolution' of regions. However, this evolution is progressively strengthening regional identity. Decentralization has not imprisoned the regions within the field of their officially defined legal competencies, but has given them the opportunity to tackle any issue of regional interest. Their legitimacy is thus based on their capacity to deal with and solve the bulk of the problems that may arise on their territory. However, this expansion dynamic is limited by the means the regions have at their disposal.

The Increase in the Means of Action of the Regions

The personnel and equipment resources transferred to the regions under the decentralization reforms were minimal when compared to what had been done for the departments. The regions had therefore to set up their own administrative structures. They usually chose to create light 'mission services' whose role was to stimulate and oversee projects rather than to manage them directly. This option was made easier by the fact that agreements made annually allow the state to put its own services at the disposal of the region for specific tasks. This approach is all the more attractive since it is free of charge (as required by the 1982-83 laws), and has been extensively used by all the regions to ensure the administrative and technical management of their programmes. Thus, when a region decides to build a secondary school, it makes use of both the rectorats (state education offices at the regional level) and the DDE (*Direction Départementale de l'Equipement*). In the same way, it uses state employment agencies when setting up professional training schemes.

The regional administration also comprises a large number of advisory bodies. Some of these are legally constituted, such as the *Conseil Economique et Social Régional* (Regional Economic and Social Council), whose scope is general, or other more specific bodies like the *Comité Régional des Prêts* (Regional Loan Committee) and the *Comité Régional de la Formation Professionnelle* (Regional Professional Training Committee). Others are created by the regional council according to need, or following an agreement between the state and the region within the framework of the planning contract (such as the follow-up committees set up to supervise joint development projects). Some of these bodies are jointly established by the state and the regions, others are purely regional. All derive from a concerted action logic.

Each region has also endowed itself with specific intervention tools to implement its policies. In the economic field these can be regional development agencies which coordinate financial bodies: *sociétés de développement régional* (regional development companies), guarantee funds and venture-capital companies. In other fields, the method most often resorted to is the creation of an association. Each region participates in a large number of organizations which make possible its cooperation with different partners in specific actions. In order to facilitate this, they form associations or *sociétés d'économie mixte* (mixed-capital companies) with partners from either the public or private sector. It is interesting to note that, in such cases, the regions resort to private law rather than creating institutions of public administration. In so doing, they have shown themselves to be very flexible, able to adapt to local (regional) needs and become very much involved in the local environment.

Most regions have tried to limit their operating budgets (sometimes, the luxury of some *hôtels de région* has been criticized – though the aim was to show the wider public that the region really existed) with a view to maximizing possibilities for regional investments (60 per cent of their overall budget). Regions have been more successful in this than departments, whose budgets are burdened with current expenditures (especially social welfare payments and salaries). Nevertheless, regional budgets are still small, despite a growth which has been more rapid than that of the state and other local authority budgets. The budgetary dimension of regions aptly epitomizes the small, but growing role regions have come to play in the French administrative system.

The regions have tried to loosen financial constraints in order to cope with the numerous applications for funding they receive. They have also sought new methods of financing projects, sometimes classical (state credit, European Union subsidies or bank loans), and sometimes more original, as in the financing of lycées in the Ile-de-France region through METPs (*Marchés d'Entreprises de Travaux Publics*).[4] Nevertheless, all regions have had to increase direct rates. The percentage of tax rates levied by the regions was at first small, but has steadily grown, thereby contributing to a 'local tax crisis'. Unfortunately, reform of the local tax system has failed to capture the interest of the legislators responsible for it (as illustrated by the recent postponement of the local income tax parliamentary bill). Therein lies the main weakness of the decentralization policy which has been implemented since 1982 and the issue which most seriously threatens its future.

CONCLUSION

Although it constitutes the newest entity of the local administrative system, the region now plays an increasingly important, and, as Gaston Defferre intended, indispensable role. Legally, the situation of regions is paradoxical: the existence of all the other categories of local authority is acknowledged by the constitution (clause 72), but the regions were created by ordinary law and keep their present status only if a subsequent ordinary law does not abrogate it. This raises the question as to whether the constitution should not be amended in order to guarantee the continued existence of the regions.

The existence of several levels of local administration create a political problem. Officially, there are three levels (municipalities, departments and regions), but the central government is now trying to promote a fourth level comprising grouped municipalities. Predictably, the local political establishment is opposing this change. The law of 6 February 1992 on the territorial administration of the Republic represents a new attempt to bring about this new fourth level which, in spite of 35 years of consistent effort, has failed to emerge. If the goals of the law are achieved, the development of inter-municipal cooperation will lead to a weakening of the departments. The cause of this is simple: since departments function increasingly as federations of municipalities which are too numerous and too weak to exercise their functions themselves, the grouping together of municipalities will make them partly redundant. Regions might then be able to take advantage of the decline of their direct competitors.

The logic of local government (which, over the period 1982-1992, has replaced that of local administration) has given the regions the capacity to deal with local problems. On the other hand, the logic of partnership submits them to numerous institutional constraints. The regions will succeed only if they manage to escape from these constraints and emerge as the main actor on the local political scene. The legitimacy they have acquired and the efficiency which they have manifested so far are the best omens for their success.

NOTES

1. The French *collèges* correspond to the English 1st to 3rd forms and the American Junior High Schools, whereas the *lycées* correspond to the English 4th to Upper 6th forms and the American High Schools (translator's note).
2. A central government body responsible for strategic planning and regional development.
3. Its legal origin is the well-known article L121-26 of the code of communes (law of 5 April 1884): 'The municipal council rules the municipality's affairs through its deliberations'. The legal interpretation is that any matter falling within the public interest of the commune has to be dealt with by the municipal council, even though there is no specific law about it.
4. These are civil engineering tenders. The civil engineering company finances the construction of the lycée itself and maintains it over a period of 10-15 years. The region pays the company on an annual basis the amounts necessary to cover these expenses. The sum the region invests is therefore smaller than in a normal tender, and the cost is spread over a longer

period of time, with the savings thus obtained hopefully compensating the increase in the financial cost of the operation.

REFERENCES

Actualité juridique. Droit administratif, 1992, Special issue. 'L'état de la décentralisation', April 1992, pp.1-152.

Albertini, J. B., Ch. Berenguer, and J. L. Marx, 1993, *Dictionnaire juridique. Pouvoirs locaux* (Paris: Dalloz).

Baguenard, J., 1973, 'L'organisation régionale (loi du 5 juillet 1972)', *Revue du droit public*, pp.1405-87.

Bourdon, J., J. M. Pontier, and J. C. Ricci, 1987, *Droit des collectivités locales* (Paris: P.U.F.).

Centre universitaire de recherches administratives et politiques de Picardie (CURAPP), 1993, *Les politiques régionales* (Paris: P.U.F).

Bourjol, M., 1970, *Région et administration régionale* (Paris: Berger-Levrault).

DATAR (Délégation à l'Aménagement du Territoire et à l'Action Régionale), 1993, *Débat National Pour l'Aménagement du Territoire. Document introductif.*

La documentation française, 1993, *Décentralisation. Bilan et perspectives.*

Dolez, B., 1993, *Coopération décentralisée et souveraineté de l'Etat: Contribution à l'étude du régime juridique de l'action extérieure des collectivités territoriales* (Lille: Editions Université de Lille 2).

Douence, J. C., 1985, 'La porte étroite. Réflexions sur la réforme du système éducatif français par la loi du 25 janvier 1985', *Revue française de droit administratif*, pp.604-23.

Douence, J. C., 1986, 'La région, collectivité à vocation générale ou spécialisée?', *Revue française de droit administratif.* pp. 539-51.

Ferrari, P., and Ch. Vier, 1972, 'La réforme régionale, loi du 5 juillet 1972', *Actualité juridique Droit administratif,* pp. 491-511.

Mabileau, A., 1991, *Le système local en France* (Paris: Montchrestien).

Madiot, J. Y., 1993, *L'aménagement du territoire* (Paris: Masson).

Millon, Ch., 1992, *Essai sur la région* (Paris: Belfond).

Moderne, F., (ed.), 1983, *La nouvelle décentralisation* (Paris: Sirey).

Moderne, F., (ed.), 1985, *Les nouvelles compétences locales* (Paris: Economica).

Muret, J. P., J. Peyré and Schmidt, 1991, *Le conseil régional* (Paris: Syros).

Nemery, J. C., 1983, 'Le nouveau régime juridique des interventions économiques des collectivités locales', *Actualité juridique. Droit administratif,* pp.65-72.

Pontier, J. M., 1993, 'La région', *Encyclopédie des collectivités locales* (Paris: Dalloz).

Pontier, J. M., *et al.*, 1986, 'La région, nouvelle collectivité locale', *Revue française de droit administratif*, pp.521-600.

Remond, B., and J. Blanc, 1993, *Les collectivités locales* (Paris: Masson).

Turpin, D., 1987, *La région* (Paris: Economica).

Vandelli, L., 1991, *Pouvoirs locaux* (Paris: Economica).

The First Regional Political Elites in France (1986-1992): A Profile

ELISABETH DUPOIRIER

As provided for by the 1982 decentralization laws, the first elections for the regional councils were held in March 1986 by direct popular vote in which 1,843 new local elites were elected to six-year terms in the 26 regions of France. Many experts believed that this initial experiment with regional democracy would be decisive for the future of the regionalization reforms. In order for this new level of politics and public administration to find a place of its own with respect to state, departmental and municipal governments, it was thought necessary that new elites, different from the local and national political leaders, should emerge. Yet, the emergence of new elites, most analysts felt, was jeopardized from the outset by the particular context in which the first regional elections were held. They were combined with the elections to the National Assembly in which national political issues overshadowed the regional dimension. The regional elections were also held according to a proportional representation system, which encouraged the dominance of the parties, and within departmental voting districts, thereby sparing party machines any serious effort to adapt the composition of their lists to the regional nature of the election. It is hard to imagine a more effective combination of obstacles to the creation of a specifically regional electoral market [*Perrineau, 1987*]. The opportunity for new personalities, connected neither with the party system nor with local *notables*, to enter the political arena was denied in practice. Following election day, most analysts, commenting on the profiles of the newly elected representatives, emphasized their lack of distinctive features with regard to traditional Fifth Republic politicians. They also feared that, as a consequence, the regional reforms might be in peril since regional councils were apparently in the clutches of local notables and partisan politics. These somewhat hasty conclusions can be disproved by examining the social profile of the new officials as well as their responses to two surveys conducted by the *Observatoire Interrégional du Politique* (OIP) [*Percheron, 1987*]. The first study was carried out when they took office in 1986, the second in 1991, the final year of their term. In terms of profile and attitudes, the first regional councillors show four original traits that will be described in succession.

GREATER PROPORTION OF SALARIED EMPLOYEES

Those who had hoped that the creation of a new political sphere would at last foster the emergence of a political body truly representative of civil society could only be disappointed by the profiles of the newly elected councillors. Yet a closer look reveals these profiles to be quite novel in comparison with other local political figures (Table 2:1). Regional councillors were in fact for the most part members of the working population (86 per cent compared with 14 per cent retired people), most of them were salaried employees (47 per cent compared with 39 per cent self-employed), and most were members of social categories characterized by a high level of education: 20 per cent were teachers and 20 per cent were professionals. This set of characteristics contrasts sharply with those of mayors, who were mainly self-employed (53 per cent), with a high concentration of farmers (36 per cent) reflecting the predominantly rural nature of most French communes. The features of regional political elites also contrast with those of departmental councillors, who include in their ranks more members from the upper social echelons (24 per cent professionals, 16 per cent teachers) than town councillors, though they remain predominantly self-employed (46 per cent) rather than salaried (37 per cent).

TABLE 2:1

COMPARISON OF THE SOCIAL BACKGROUND OF MAYORS, DEPARTMENTAL COUNCILLORS, AND REGIONAL COUNCILLORS

	Mayors elected in 1983	Departmental councillors elected 1985	Regional councillors elected 1986
Self-employed	53%	46%	39%
Farmers	36%	10%	6%
Indstrialists, tradesmen, craftsmen	12%	12%	13%
Professionals	5%	24%	20%
Private sector employees	14%	13%	17%
Public sector employees	13%	24%	30%
Teachers	8%	16%	20%
Other civil servants	5%	8%	10%
Retired	20%	17%	14%

Source: ADJA Statistics published by La Documentation Française.

Certainly, the new regional councillors were no more representative of society than their counterparts in other local elected assemblies. The over-representation of public sector employees compared with those from the private sector is a noteworthy distortion, probably explained by the greater availability of the former to take up political office. They may also be better prepared for the increasingly technical nature of community management than other local councillors drawn from the private sector.

A HIGHLY POLITICIZED ELITE COMPARED WITH LOCAL POLITICAL OFFICE-HOLDERS

Given the 1986 electoral conditions, it is perhaps unsurprising that elected regional councillors were highly politicized in comparison with their counterparts in the *conseils généraux* (departmental councils) (Table 2: 2). The first survey undertaken by the OIP shows that in 1986 practically all of them were members of one of the political groups in the regional council (93 per cent) and this remained true in 1991 (92 per cent). In contrast, this was true of considerably fewer departmental councillors (75 per cent). In addition to their duties within the regional council, in 1991 regional councillors continued to hold positions of responsibility within their party, particularly at a local level (66 per cent), but also at the regional (44 per

TABLE 2:2
PARTISAN CHARACTER OF REGIONAL ELITES COMPARED WITH
DEPARTMENTAL ELITES

	Regional councillors (1)	Departmental councillors (2)
Private involvement		
Party membership	92%	75%
Belongs to a political grouping in the Council	94%	75%
Follows party line in council votes		
'Always'	31%	17%
'In most cases'	62%	61%
Party or institutional closeness		
Closer to another councillor whatever his party affiliation	33%	49%
Closer to a deputy or senator with the same political affinity	58%	42%

Notes: (1) OIP 1986 survey
(2) OIP/APCG 1991 survey

cent) and national (31 per cent) levels. For some elected officials, especially Union for French Democracy (UDF) and National Front (FN) members, the regional mandate serves as a springboard to further a party career at the national level (only 27 per cent of them had such responsibilities at the time of their election).

This widespread partisanship is expressed by near unanimous support (93 per cent) for the principle of following the party line in council votes: 31 per cent fully endorsed it, and 62 per cent defended the principle 'in most cases'. By comparison, only 17 per cent of the departmental councillors advocated voting systematically along party lines, (though 61 per cent abided by it 'in most cases'). The final indicator of 'overpoliticization' is that allegiance to the party is regarded as considerably more important than institutional solidarity. Fifty-eight per cent of regional councillors felt 'closer to a deputy or a senator with the same political affinity' than 'to another regional councillor whatever his party affiliation'. This stand on principle is again strictly inverted for departmental councillors who more commonly (49 per cent) prefer institutional to political solidarity.

It is true that this image of highly politicized elites who are closely integrated into the party apparatus applies especially to the younger councillors: a new generation of '*quadras*' (those in their forties), often holding few offices concurrently – 40 per cent of them have only a regional mandate – who have served their political apprenticeship in the offices of mayors and chairpersons of departmental or regional councils. Their party activities supplement this experience: 34 per cent (instead of an average 27 per cent of regional councillors generally) have responsibilities in their party's national bureau and often perform these duties concurrently with responsibilities at the regional and local level (21 per cent instead of an average 13 per cent). Their career profile is indeed one of a new elite, quite detached from the traditional networks of local *notables* to which their elders generally belong. Within the regional councils, this new generation of politicians coexists alongside political dignitaries with more traditional traits: relatively aged (over 55), holding several offices, usually including mayor of a rural commune (46 per cent) or a seat on the departmental council (33 per cent). These individuals of a previous generation are, however, less involved than the average regional councillor in the party machinery (31 per cent as opposed to nine per cent have no position of political responsibility in a party). They - like their departmental counterparts - are also more inclined to choose institutional solidarity over party allegiance.

A REGIONAL IDENTITY FORGED BY EXPERIENCE IN OFFICE

The OIP surveys also reveal the gradual emergence of a regional identity among the new elites. Immediately after being elected, regional councillors were cautious regarding the significance of their mandate and the future of the region. After six years on the job, however, their experience convinced them of the region's chances of achieving recognition in the French political landscape. Through a process of institutional socialization the doubts and reservations that bridled their commitment were overcome. Three indicators attest to this change (Table 2:3).

The first is an indicator of attachment to the regional mandate. In 1986, only one-third of the newly elected representatives holding several offices concurrently cited regional councillor as their preferred office. Six years

TABLE 2:3
THE EMERGENCE OF A REGIONAL IDENTITY

	1986	1991	Diff. 91/86
Preferred office of regional councillor			
Mayor, deputy mayor, town councillor	42%	28%	-14
Regional councillor	32%	57%	+25
Departmental councillor	11%	7%	-4
Deputy, senator, European deputy	2%	5%	+3
– No Answer (NA)	13%	3%	-10
Adminstrative and political unit of the future			
The region	54%	90%	+36
The department	41%	8%	-33
– NA	5%	2%	-3
Most important figure in implementing the policy of decentralization			
Regional council president	45%	63%	+18
Departmental council president	26%	17%	-9
National legislator	10%	10%	–
The prefect	2%	6%	+4
Mayor of the regional capital	2%	1%	-3
– NA	16%	3%	-13

Source: 1986 and 1991 OIP surveys of regional councillors.

later, priority attachment to this office was expressed by 57 per cent of representatives who are still regional councillors. This explicit preference for the post of regional councillor holds true regardless of the councillors' party allegiance and the number of offices held. It is, however, all the stronger when the officials belong to political groups governing the regions. This suggests that exercising institutional responsibilities plays a determining role in explaining personal commitment to the position of regional councillor.

The second indicator of the emergence of a regional identity is the strengthening of the officials' confidence with regard to the future of the region. Here again the evolution of opinion between the 1986 and the 1991 surveys is striking. When they took office, the new regional elites were sceptical about whether the region would in the long run win over the department as an administrative and political unit: a slight majority (54 per cent) believed from the start in the future of the region, but a strong minority (41 per cent) declared itself convinced of the department's supremacy. The new elites' forecasts were more pessimistic at that time than those of the voters who much more clearly predicted a bright regional future (59 per cent compared with 25 per cent). Yet, after six years in office, the regional representatives opted clearly in favour of the region and the nearly unanimous trust they placed in its future (90 per cent compared to eight per cent trust in the department) greatly surpasses the confidence, however solid, demonstrated by the public in the region (70 per cent compared with 21 per cent).

Lastly, confidence in the capacity of the chairperson of the regional council to implement the policy of decentralization has increased. He is now considered by 66 per cent of regional councillors as the 'most important figure', preferred over the departmental council chairperson in whom only 17 per cent of councillors still primarily placed their trust in 1991.

ELITES UPHOLDING A COMMON IDEA OF REGIONALIZATION

The last conclusion drawn from the OIP surveys concerns the ambition and realism of the new elites regarding the region. Upon taking office, officials clearly indicated their intention to hold the state at a respectful distance from the new regional power: 61 per cent as opposed to 38 per cent declared themselves dissatisfied with the balance of power between the state and the region provided by the legislation. Not counting officials elected on a socialist ticket (logically inclined to defend the content of decentralization laws instituted by the socialist government), dissatisfaction was expressed by over two-thirds of elected regional officials. This dissatisfaction contrasts with the positive attitude (58 per cent compared with 38 per cent) with which the departmental councillors at that time regarded the balance of power between state and department set forth in the same decentralization laws. A phenomenon that correlates with the previous one is the following: in 1991, the councillors were more than ever devoted to furthering the policy of decentralization and regionalization. Sixty-nine per cent of them were in favour of the policy in 1986, whilst 86 per cent shared this opinion at the end of their term. Moreover, socialist councillors (who were in opposition in all but two regions at this time) proved to be as enthusiastic about the region as their fellow councillors from other parties.

This ambition is nevertheless accompanied by a very realistic conception of the functions that should be devolved to the regional council. Unlike their voters, who support a conception of the 'welfare region' intervening in all areas that affect their priority concerns (social security, law and order, employment), the regional councillors (out of political realism or respect for the functions of other public authorities?) advanced gingerly upon taking office and requested a broadening of their powers only in those areas in which the legislation empowered them to act: professional training, environment, education, and road networks.

Six years of experience in the regional councils and a context of deepening economic recession made them even more wary in 1991 about enlarging their capacities, particularly to cover matters of taxation and social security. Their priorities still lay in devoting themselves to the tasks set forth by the 1982 legislation. Thirty-seven per cent (28 per cent in 1986) felt that professional training was the most urgent regional task and 53 per cent named it as the most important means of solving employment problems in the region (33 per cent in 1986). On the priority and urgency of the problem, elected officials and voters were once again in harmony.

CONCLUSION

Do we now have new elites for new regions? From a sociological perspective one might be tempted to give an affirmative answer. In terms of social background, the first regional councillors were more in touch with civil society and better qualified to manage this new local community than the departmental and particularly municipal elites. From a political perspective, the first regional councillors were also people with experience and more solidly anchored in the party system than their departmental and municipal counterparts. This was to be expected given the conditions in which they were elected (notably, the particular proportional representation system, which encouraged the dominance of the party system). In sum, they were professional politicians with contrasting political identities.

Yet beyond the divergences, six years of institutional responsibility have plainly fostered a convergence of views on the status and the role of the region. Contrary to the fears expressed in 1986 by the majority of political observers, politicization did not smother regionalization. The first regional elites have indeed been bearers of regional autonomy. The process of institutional socialization turned out to be strong enough to surmount, to the benefit of the region, the hesitations and doubts voiced at the beginning of the mandate. Drawing up a typology of regional officials in 1986, Annick Percheron opposed 'regionalists' to 'departmentalists' and 'the undecided'. By the end of the term, the departmentalists and the undecided have largely disappeared. The regional experience has taken shape through action.

REFERENCES

Percheron, A., (ed.), 1987, *La Région An 1* (Paris: P.U.F., Collection du GRAL).
Perrineau, P., (ed.), 1987, *Régions - Le Baptême des Urnes* (Paris: Pédone).
Rondin, A., 1985, *Le sacre des notables* (Paris: Fayard).

The Finances of the French Regions in Retrospect

GUY GILBERT

Since 1982, France has occupied a singular position in the European Community with respect to the territorial organization of the state. In most unitary states such as the United Kingdom, Ireland, Denmark or the Netherlands, there are two tiers of government. In federal states such as Germany or Belgium, or in states with strong regional governments such as Spain and Italy, there exist three tiers of government, with the middle-level tier (the German Länder, Italian and Belgian Regions and Spanish Autonomous Communities) being responsible for tasks formerly undertaken by the central level of government. With three tiers of local government (36,500 *communes*, 90 *départements* and 22 *régions*) France occupies an ambiguous position: its governmental structure remains unitary, but the territorial organization of the state is quite similar to that of federal countries.

This situation has important implications for public finances. On the one hand, this 'proliferation' of fiscal tiers in France could, in theory, favour the efficient allocation of responsibilities between various levels of government. It could also strengthen a sort of 'competitive federalism' between the regions and the departments. On the other hand, it undoubtedly complicates the allocation of responsibilities as well as the distribution of fiscal powers and other financial means between different local authorities. In this situation, some co-financing of public activities is unavoidable. This practice could, in turn, result in more 'fiscal illusion' and more fiscal waste, thereby hindering an efficient allocation of local public goods. The so-called 'proliferation' of local government is also important from a political viewpoint. In particular, it is often argued that this situation does not necessarily enhance either the transparency of local collective choices (the 'accountability' issue), or local democracy.

The fiscal behaviour of French regions is often regarded as 'irresponsible' compared with the alleged 'virtuous' behaviour of the departments. The fiscal implications of the creation of regions are therefore of particular importance. The 1982-86 decentralisation laws concentrated more on the distribution of responsibilities than on ensuring an appropriate distribution of tax bases between municipalities, departments and regions. Consequently, there was no correlation between the 'spending needs' for functions allocated to local authorities and the financial resources of the latter. State fiscal transfers to the regions, designed to compensate them for increased expenditures did not, in fact, resolve this mismatch between responsibilities and resources. The evolution of the regions' finances over time clearly illustrates this fiscal imbalance.

The first section of this article presents an overview of the evolution of regional finances in France. The 'explosion' of regional budgets since 1982 must be placed in the context of their small size compared with those of the departments and municipalities, which together account for the majority of local authority expenditure. The second section highlights the changing role of French regions by means of an analysis of the expenditure side of their budgets. This study confirms that since the 1970s, the regions have acquired more and more responsibilities, especially in the fields of education, training, and economic planning. The third section focuses upon regional fiscal resources. Contrary to the widespread view that regions have been fiscally irresponsible, it is argued that, generally speaking, they have consistently faced budgetary constraints which have necessitated the permanent balancing of various types of resources, taxes and loans. The concluding section elaborates on the possible future development of French regional finances within the European context. Three scenarios are briefly presented, which illustrate both the necessity of a local tax reform defining the rules of the fiscal game for local governments, and the limited room for manoeuvre which exists on such matters.

THE EVOLUTION OF FRENCH REGIONS' BUDGETS: SHARP INCREASES,
BUT SMALL BUDGETS

In 1993, total local public expenditure (of regions, departments and municipalities - APUL), amounted to around 10 per cent of GNP and 47 per cent of central state expenditure. The regional share of the total remains marginal (4.7 per cent of the APUL expenditure in 1993), but has rapidly increased since 1974, the year in which the predecessors to the present regional authorities (the *établissements publics régionaux* - EPRs) were created. Indeed, the 1992 regional expenditure levels were 36 times greater than those of the EPRs in 1974. Interestingly, the rate of increase in regional expenditure has also been quite irregular over time. In the early period (1974-1981), the growth rate remained low and stable: the EPR budgets accounted for less than one per cent of the APUL (Table 3:1).

During the second period (1982-86), new, financially significant, responsibilities were gradually transferred to the regions. In consequence, regional expenditure exploded: the average annual rate of growth reached 45 per cent in real terms throughout this period, compared with the five per cent

TABLE 3:1
REGIONAL EXPENDITURES: 1979-1992[1][2]
(IN CONSTANT FRANCS 1992)

Expenditure (mil.F 1977)	1979	1980	1982	1983	1984	1985	1986	1987	1988	1989	1990	1991	1992
Current exp.	332	387	846	2923	5102	6190	9147	9977	10723	11153	12455	13748	15044
Capital exp.	4699	4423	6080	6973	7160	8522	9607	12044	15044	18332	20679	24943	26217
TOTAL	5031	4810	6926	9896	12262	14712	18754	22021	25767	29484	33134	38691	41261
Annual Rate of increase(%)													
Current exp.	18	17	71	245	75	21	48	9	7	4	12	10	9
Capital exp.	4	-6	11	15	3	19	13	25	25	22	13	21	5
TOTAL	5	-4	16	43	24	20	27	17	17	14	12	17	7
Structure of exp.													
Current exp. (%)	7	8	12	30	42	42	49	45	42	38	38	36	36
Capital exp. (%)	93	92	88	70	58	58	51	55	58	62	62	64	64
TOTAL	100	100	100	100	100	100	100	100	100	100	100	100	100

Source: GILBERT (1991) and MARCHAND (various years) DGCL (1994).
   (1) Expenditures = Current expenditures + capital expenditures + current surplus
   (2) excluding Ile-de-France and overseas Regions.

annual rate of increase in expenditure for other levels of local government. Thus, the regional share of total public expenditures increased to four per cent in 1986. This 'sky-rocketing' increase progressively slowed down at the end of the 1980s, though the rate of increase in regional expenditure remains somewhat higher than that of the departments and municipalities. As a result, in 1992, regional expenditure amounted to 4.9 per cent of total local government expenditure. This sum amounted to only 960 Francs per capita compared with 3,400 Francs per capita for departmental expenditure and 6,600 Francs per capita for municipal expenditure. These aggregate figures are to some extent misleading; regional disparities in expenditure levels per capita must also be taken into account. For 1992, the figures vary from 688F/inh. in the Lorraine region to 1,176 F/inh. in the Haute-Normandie region. No simple explanation of such regional disparities can be provided. In part, such differences often appear to be due to special local circumstances. Yet, even allowing for these differences, there has been a general upward trend in regional expenditure everywhere, which probably is a result of common factors.

STRUCTURAL TRENDS IN REGIONS' EXPENDITURES

Two basic structural features help to explain the increase in French regional expenditure since 1983 (see Table 3:2). First, the substitution of current expenditures for capital expenditure, as a consequence of the transfer of new responsibilities to the regions. Second, the substantial expenditure needs of these particular policy areas (notably, education and training) where the

TABLE 3:2
REGIONAL BUDGETS: 1980–1993
BILLIONS OF F.F., AND % OF EXPENDITURES OR RESOURCES

	1980	1987	1989	1991[1]	1993[1]
Total expenditures	5 billions	28,4 b.	40,5 b.	50,3 b.	60,7 b.
Currrent expenditures	10%	43,9%	35,3%	31%	33%
Incl. (salaries)	(0,8%)	(2%)	(1,9%)	(0,9%)	(1,2%)
(interests)	(5,9%)	(5,7%)	(4,5%)	(2%)	(3,2%)
(subsidies)	(1,4%)	(32,4%)	(25,5%)	(12,9%)	(16,2%)
Capital expenditures Incl.	90%	56,1%	64,7%	69%	67%
(Debt Repayment)	(4,1%)	(4,6%)	(5,5%)	(2,1%)	(2,4%)
(Gross Investment)	(1,2%)	(10,8%)	(18,6%)	(12,9%)	(16,2%)
(Subsidies in capital)	(71,7%)	(35%)	(30,6%)	(34,5%)	(40,1%)
Total incomes	5,3 billions	29,4 b.	40,5 b.	48,9 b.	60,7 b.
	100%	100%	100%	100%	100%
Tax resources	65,7%	53,2%	52,9%	50%	49%
Incl. (direct tax)	(28,4%)	(23,4%)	(24,9%)	n.a.	n.a.
Subsidies	12,5%	30,1%	30,6%	29%	27%
Borrowings	14,2%	11%	11,1%	14%	13%
Miscellaneous incomes	7,6%	4,7%	5,4%	7%	11%

Source: Computed out of Ministry of Interior and Ministry of Finances (1992) data and Crédit Local de France.

(1) overseas regions excluded.

central state had invested too little in the past and had therefore transferred potential 'deficits' to the regions.

At the time of their creation, the EPRs were basically given responsibility to implement central government operations on a territorial basis and to rationalize within a regional framework the regional operations involved in the national plan, which was determined by the central government. In budgetary terms, the EPRs received transfers from the central government and redistributed them in the form of specific grants and capital subsidies. Compared with these transfer flows, EPR current expenditure levels remained of limited importance. The budgetary powers of the EPRs were strictly limited by the imposition of a ceiling (set by the central government) on regional fiscal resources. Moreover, the capital operations financed by the EPR capital subsidies were in reality mostly co-financed and ultimately controlled by the central government [*Hertzog, 1991*].

However, following the 1982 decentralization reforms the structure of regional expenses changed rapidly: the proportion of current expenditure increased from 12 per cent of total regional expenditure in 1982 to 50 per cent in 1986. This structural trend has progressively been reversed since 1986. In recent years, capital expenditure levels have once again increased due to important regional investment programmes for schools. The present structure of regional expenditure is thus, two-thirds capital expenditure, and one-third current expenditure. At the same time, the very nature of capital expenditure has changed significantly. A decade ago, EPR capital expenditure mainly consisted of subsidies to other local authorities or miscellaneous public entities. Since 1986, however, direct capital investment has progressively replaced regional subsidies and now account for two-thirds of total regional, capital expenditure. These direct investments have been used mainly for building and maintaining schools and colleges but also, albeit to a lesser extent, for improving and extending the buildings of the regional administration itself. This latter point has been often criticized by the regions' opponents as the very epitome of waste.

The increase in capital expenditure and the shift towards more direct investment are not the only causes of the explosion in regional expenditure. Another source of increase in regional expenditure can be found in the evolution of current expenditure. Since 1977, per capita current expenditure by French regions has increased thirteen-fold in real terms. In absolute terms, however, the contribution of current expenditure to the growth of total regional expenditure remains of minor importance: in 1990 current regional expenditure per capita amounted to just 36F/inh. Turning to more specific sources of expenditure, special attention must be paid to the financial impact of the regions having assumed responsibility in 1983 for vocational training, and then in 1986 for the construction, maintenance and expansion of secondary school buildings. By way of financial compensation for these new responsibilities, the regions received a special subsidy, equal in value to the amounts the central government formerly devoted to these items (more details on these specific subsidies are given in the following section of this paper). Subsequently, however, actual regional expenditure on training increased sharply in volume from 35F/inh. in 1983 to 78 F/inh. in 1989 (in 1983 F. Francs), when it accounted for some 13 per cent of total regional expenditures (see Table 3:3).

Investment in secondary education constitutes a major source of regional expenditure; by 1992 it accounted for one third of the regions' budgets,

TABLE 3:3
TRAINING AND APPRENTICESHIP: EXPENDITURES AND RESOURCES
OF REGIONS 1983–1992

	1983	1984	1985	1986	1987	1988	1989	1990	1991	1992[1]
Expenditures										
• volume										
mil.F.1977) 1522		2976	3275	3426	2433	3616	3445	3912	4200	4651
• volume										
per capita	35	68	74	78	78	82	78	n.a.	n.a.	n.a.
• % in total										
regional exp.	16	26	24	19	17	15	13	n.a.	n.a.	n.a.
Resources										
• volume										
(mil.F.1977)	369	1673	1766	1834	1937	2088	2165	n.a.	n.a.	n.a.
• volume per										
capita	8	38	40	42	44	47	49	n.a.	n.a.	n.a.
• ratio resources:										
exp(%)	24	56	54	54	56	58	63	n.a.	n.a.	n.a.

Source: GILBERT (1991) and MARCHAND, (various years) and DGCL (1993).
    (1) provisional

averaging 332 F/inh. The annual rate of increase in educational investment
by regions is also higher than for any other category of expenditure. This
increased at an average rate of 39 per cent per year over the period 1986-
1991. However, this diminished over time from + 46 per cent for 1988/87,
to + 45 per cent for 1989/88, + 33 per cent for 1990/1989 and to only +23
per cent for 1991/90. These impressive figures can be explained partly by
the severe need for the (re)construction of schools, but also in terms of the
political preferences of regional councillors. As a matter of fact, sharp
differences exist between regions in this respect. For example, the Ile-de-
France region presents the highest rate of increase (+ 50 per cent per annum
on average over the period 1986-1991). Thus, the major shifts in the
structure of French regional expenditure between 1982 and 1992 reflect the
new responsibilities given to the regions as well as the weight of local
preferences and constraints. Massive direct interventions in the field of
training or education have led to increased capital and current expenditure.

THE MANAGEMENT OF REGIONS' RESOURCES

Alongside the shift in the structure of regional expenditure structure,
regional incomes have also undergone important changes with respect to the
balance between taxes and subsidies.

The basic structure of regional incomes has remained fairly stable over
time. In 1989, for instance, current resources (taxes + subsidies) accounted

TABLE 3:4
SECONDARY EDUCATION: THE REGIONS' BUDGETS (ILE-DE-FRANCE AND OVERSEAS REGIONS EXCLUDED) (1986–1992)

	1986			1987			1988			1989			1990			1991			1992		
	(1)	(2)	total	(1)	(2)	total	(1)	(2)	total	(1)	(2)	total	(1)	(2)	total	(1)	(2)	total	(1)	(2)	total
Expenditures																					
• mill.francs	1951	971	2922	2345	2803	5148	2453	4677	7130	2592	6382	8974	2706	9480	12186	2941	12133	15074	3180	12176	15336
• exp.per capita	44,3	22,1	66,4	53,2	63,7	116,9	55,7	106,2	161,9	58,9	145,	203,9	61,5	215,3	276,8	64	266	330	69	265	336
• %in tot. reg.exp.	25	12	18	26	26	26	25	34	30	24,9	37,3	32,6	23	48	38	22	49	40	21	46	37
Resources																					
• millions francs	1771	541	2312	2124	1291	3415	2189	2253	4442	2368	2532	4900	2558	2972	5530	2673	3758	6431	2890	3900	6720
• exp.per capita	40,2	12,3	52,5	48,2	29,3	77,6	49,7	51,2	100,9	53,8	57,5	111,3	58,1	67,6	125,6	58	82	141	63	85	147
• ratio res/exp(%)	90,7	55,7	79,1	90,6	46,1	66,3	89,2	48,2	62,3	91,4	39,7	54,6	94,5	31,4	46,4	90,9	31,0	42,7	91,5	32,0	43,8

Source: Gilbert (1991) and Marchand (mis. years), DGCL (1993).
(1) current expenditures
(2) capital expenditure

TABLE 3:5
FISCAL RESOURCES OF REGIONS 1977–1989

Fiscal resources (mil.F. 1977)	1979	1982	1983	1984	1985	1986	1987	1988	1989
• Current res.	2849	4452	7365	9926	10904	13717	16919	18291	20627
• Capital res.	543	1925	2811	2640	2537	3584	4851	5651	7116
Total	3392	6377	10177	12565	13441	17301	21770	23942	27744
Annual rate of increase % *Annual rate of increase %*									
• Current res.	5	11	65	35	10	26	23	8	13
• Capital res.	-24	47	46	-6	-4	41	35	16	26
Total	-1	20	60	23	7	29	26	10	16
Structure of resources (%) *Structure of resources(%)*									
• Current res.	84	70	72	79	81	79	78	76	74
• Capital res.	16	30	28	21	19	21	22	24	26
Total	100	100	100	100	100	100	100	100	100

Source: Gilbert (1991) and Marchand (various years).

for about 75 per cent of total income compared with 84 per cent in 1977 (see Tables 3:4 and 3:5). However, during the same period, the regional tax system and the system of regional subsidies changed significantly.

REGIONAL TAXES

As is the case for the municipalities and departments, the French Constitution does not allow the regions to set up new taxes. This is the exclusive prerogative of the central government. By implication, the latter is also responsible for ensuring there is an approximate balance between regional expenditures and the tax receipts available to regions under 'normal' tax rates. *A priori*, it appears that this has been achieved. The 1982 decentralization laws transferred to the regions exclusive, indirect taxes in addition to the same direct tax bases as the other local governments, so as to enable them to meet their new financial obligations more easily. Before 1988, regional direct taxation consisted of a regional additional tax (*taxe régionale additionnelle* – TRA) levied in all regions (apart from Ile-de-France where the TRA was replaced by a *taxe speciale d'équipement* – TSE

– earmarked for investment projects). Though optional, all regions in fact made use of the TRA, which was an additional tax, levied on the four traditional sources of local authority fiscal income set by the communes and the departments. These included the *taxe d'habitation* (TH), a housing tax based on rental income; *taxes foncières sur les propriétés bâties* (TFPB) and *taxes foncières sur les propriétés non bâties*, (TFBNB); two property taxes based on the official market value of buildings and land; and the *taxe professionnelle* (TP), a business tax based on the value-added (calculated on a factor-costs basis) by businesses and professionals. The TRA was thus a composite tax, but regions determined the level of each of the four individual taxes (TH, TFPB, TFPNB, TP), in the same way as departments have traditionally done. The TRA receipts were also subject to a ceiling imposed by the central government. However, as a result of two reforms in 1986 and 1988, regional direct taxation is now quite similar in structure to that of the departments and municipalities. The fiscal ceiling mentioned above has been removed and regional councils freely vote separate rates for each of the four tax bases (TH, TFPB, TFPNB, and TP). The Ile-de-France region remains a special case.

Conversely, the structure of regional indirect taxes have been reformed in depth. The regions, were initially given the right to impose taxes formerly levied by the central government, so as to compensate regions for the new compulsory obligations they had acquired in the decentralization process. These new regional taxes included the following:

• A registration fee (*carte grise*) on car vehicles registered within the regional territory. This tax is paid by car owners and the level is set by the region. It may be either a uniform charge, or proportional to the engine capacity of the vehicle.
• A tax on car licences issued within the region. This is a uniform charge (set by the region) levied on all licence applicants.
• An additional tax on property transactions (which is, in fact, an additional tax to the *taxe de publicité foncière*) and registration fees related to such transactions. The (uniform) rate is submitted to a ceiling (set at 1.6 per cent of the sale value).

In Corsica and Ile-de-France, the provisions relating to indirect taxation were slightly different. In Corsica, the region (and not the two constituent departments) also receives the *vignette* receipts (an annual tax on car vehicles). In Ile-de-France, the region also levies an additional tax to the Municipal Equipement Tax (TLE) at a uniform rate of one per cent.

In quantitative terms, the structure of regional taxation has changed significantly over time (see Table 3:6). First, the importance of direct

TABLE 3:6
STRUCTURE OF REGIONAL TAX RESOURCES
(MILLIONS FRANCS 1992)

	1979	1982	1983	1984	1985	1986	1987	1988	1989	1990	1991	1992
Direct taxes	1473	1908	2868	3944	4443	4914	6890	7720	9696	11365	12453	13111
Indirect taxes	2644	2706	4347	4580	4955	5355	6322	6797	7186	8528	7927	7665
Total	4117	4514	7215	8524	9398	10269	13212	14517	16882	19893	20380	20776

Source: Gilbert (1991) and Marchand (various years).

regional taxes has increased. Direct taxes accounted for only 37 per cent of total fiscal income in 1979. However, by 1989, this figure had risen to 57 per cent. Direct regional tax receipts per capita thus increased from 34F in 1984 to 360F in 1989. The rate of increase in direct tax receipts (20 per cent per year on average over the period 1974-1982) was nearly twice that of municipalities and departments, whose income from direct taxes grew at an average rate of 12 per cent per annum during the same period. However, the rate of increase in regional direct taxation tended to slow down after 1989. During the year 1990 to 1991, for instance, regional revenue from direct taxes grew by only 13 per cent.

Meanwhile, the structure of the regional direct tax receipts has remained fairly constant: revenue from the *taxe professionnelle* (TP) accounts for roughly half of direct regional taxation; the *taxe d'habitation* (TH), for a quarter with revenue from the two property taxes contributing the remaining quarter. The increase in the direct taxes receipts reflects an increase in the tax rates (levied by the region), rather than an increase in the tax bases. Only

TABLE 3:7
NOMINAL DIRECT TAXES: REGIONAL RATES

	1980	1981	1982	1983	1984	1985	1986
Tax on built property							
(TFBP)	0,384	0,375	0,413	0,522	0,580	0,672	0,702
Land tax (TFPNB)	0,977	1,060	1,260	1,700	2,390	2,450	2,550
Housing tax (TH)	0,353	0,345	0,369	0,458	0,566	0,576	0,597
Tax on business (TP)	0,392	0,366	0,399	0,567	0,627	0,626	0,654
	1987	1988	1989	1990	1991	1992	
Tax on built property							
(TFBP)	0,896	0,945	1,196	1,329	1,34	1,38	
Land tax 9TFPNB)	3,620	3,780	4,440	4,830,	4,70	4,70	
Housing tax (TH)	0,746	0,798	0,971	1,083	1,10	1,12	
Tax on business (TP)	0,938	0,981	1,187	1,327	1,35	1,39	

Source: Gilbert (1991) and Marchand (various years).

25 per cent of the increase in total tax receipts can be attributed to the growth of the tax bases (especially in the case of the TH and TP) (see Table 3:7).

This pattern clearly illustrates the relative lack of elasticity of direct tax bases over time and the resulting upward pressure on the rates. The average, annual increase in regional direct tax rates between 1980 and 1990 was 25 per cent (for the TH), 39 per cent (for the TFPNB), two per cent (for the TFBP) and 24 per cent (for the TP). By comparison, direct tax rates increased, on average by just two per cent per year in the municipalities and departments.

In this situation, indirect taxes remain vital for regional governments. They represented 40 per cent of total fiscal revenue for the regions in 1992. In terms of volume, the annual rate of increase in indirect income actually fell from 5.5 per cent during the early period, 1974-1982 to 4.4 per cent during the period 1982-1989. This was due to both the transfer of regional tax bases and the increase in the rates of direct taxation. The structure of indirect taxation has also undergone major changes. Until 1982, the tax on property transactions predominated, accounting for 61 per cent of total indirect taxes for 1981. However, after the decentralisation laws, the share of the car licence and car registration fees increased and together accounted for 65 per cent of total indirect regional fiscal income in 1990.

The explosion of regional taxes raises once again the question of the optimal degree of liberty which should be left to the regions on fiscal matters. It has often pointed out (see *Labie: 1991; Conseil des Impôts: 1990*) that regions have been quick to exploit to the full all new fiscal opportunities granted to them. Thus regions have lost little time in exercising their right to increase tax rates and/or award tax deductions and rebates. It has also been noted that as the ceiling on direct regional tax rates was removed (bringing regions in line with departments), the gap between the most heavily and the least heavily taxed regions tended to grow significantly. This was especially true for direct regional tax levels. However, the question as to whether such fiscal behaviour constitutes definitive proof of the 'fiscal irresponsibility' of the French regions is debatable.

REGIONAL SUBSIDIES

The subsidies received by the regions amounted to 12.5 per cent of total regional resources in 1980, rising to 30.6 per cent in 1989, before falling to 27 per cent in 1993. More than 80 per cent of this sharp increase resulted from new subsidies created in 1984 and 1986, intended to compensate regions for the costs of additional responsibilities transferred to them by the 1982 reforms. Responsibility for vocational training and apprenticeships was transferred to the regions on 1 June 1983, other miscellaneous responsibilities on 1 January 1984, and responsibility for secondary schools on 1 January 1986. In principle, these new responsibilities transferred to the regions were to be financed jointly (in equal parts) by the transfer of indirect taxes (see above) and, by a block grant, the *Dotation Globale de Décentralisation* (DGD). A large part of the DGD relates to regional expenditures on training. It is calculated on the basis of the previous year's DGD, together with a set of 'needs' indicators – regional unemployment, population, size, number of apprentices in 1982, average length of training programme per capita in 1982 [*Marchand, 1987a*].

Two further subsidies were also created to compensate the regions for expenditure on secondary education. Current expenditure on schools was to be financed out of the DGD on the basis of the reported costs. Investment costs are financed by a *Dotation Régionale d'Equipement Scolaire* (DRES) which was introduced in 1986. This is distributed among the regions on the basis of the capacity of existing schools, the size of the school-age population and the state of the buildings. Each region is guaranteed a minimum annual increase in the DRES [*Marchand, 1991*].

In reality, the transfer of fiscal resources to the regions has not fully compensated regions for the costs they have incurred with respect to their responsibilities in the fields of vocational training and school buildings. The main cause of the deficit is the high cost of building and maintaining secondary education establishments. In 1986, just one year after the transfer of this responsibility to the regions, the deficit amounted to 20 per cent of total regional expenditure on secondary education, a figure which rose to 38 per cent in 1988 [*Marchand, 1991*]. Five regions have financed nearly half of their expenditure on education out of their own resources. At least two reasons help to explain this phenomenon. The first is that increases in the DGD have been limited by the fact that the size of this subsidy is linked to increases in the GDP. The second relates to the poor state of the school buildings inherited by the regions. This situation was due to the failure on the part of the central state to invest in school construction/repairs in the year preceding the transfer of responsibilities. In 1986, central state investment expenditure on secondary schools amounted to less than one billion francs. In 1991, the regions collectively spent 15.5 billion francs on secondary school construction and maintenance.

REGIONAL BORROWING

The accumulated debt of the French regions reached 15 billion francs in 1989 and was estimated to be 21 billion francs in 1991 (see Table 3:8).

The level of debt per capita increased from 13F in 1977 to 338F in 1989, 479F in 1991 and 582F in 1992. However, the amount of debt per capita

TABLE 3:8
REGIONS' PUBLIC DEBT
(MILLIONS CURRENT FRANCS)

	1977	1978	1979	1980	1981	1982	1983	1984
Borrowings	120	197	364	340	646	1202	1989	1980
Stock of debt	578	721	1018	1274	1819	2914	4776	6566
Debt per capita	13	16	23	29	41	66	108	149
	1985	1986	1987	1988	1989	1990	1991	1992
Borrowings	1937	2327	2592	2330	3473	3396	6274	9666
Stock of debt	8241	10021	11778	12661	14863	18998	21886	30017
Debt per capita	187	228	268	288	338	386	479	582

Source: Gilbert (1991) and Marchand (various years) DGCL (1993).

remains very low, compared with the indebtedness of the departments (1,678 F per capita in 1989) or that of the municipalities (4,316 F per capita in 1989). The pattern of regional debt also appears rather chaotic. After 1981, indebtedness rose rapidly: the rate of increase accelerated between 1981 and 1984 following the decentralisation process. It slowed down between 1985 and 1988, but then accelerated again. There are many reasons

TABLE 3:9
RATIO: ANNUAL DEBT BURDEN/CURRENT RESOURCES
(ALL FRENCH REGIONS)

	1977	1978	1979	1980	1981	1982	1983	1984
Debt Burden [1]	86	108	136	182	230	309	494	813
Inlc.								
. interests	41	54	70	98	129	203	367	623
. Reimb.in.cap.	44	54	67	84	101	106	127	190
Debt burden/ cur.res (%)	6,6	6,9	7,5	8,4	9,2	8,3	9,5	11,1
	1985	1986	1987	1988	1989	1990	1991	1992
Debt Burden [1]	1089	1580	1915	2772	2624	2792	3064	3672
Inlc.								
. interests	826	1034	1080	1325	1353	1471	1877	2138
. Reimb.in.cap.	263	546	835	1447	1271	1261	1387	1536
Debt burden/ cur.res (%)	11,1	12,5	12,0	15,6	12,7	11,2	11,7	13,6

Source: Gilbert (1991) and Marchand (various years) DGCL (1993).

for this pattern. First, there is the time lag between the transfer of fiscal resources and fiscal needs. Second, regions have limited room for manoeuvre with regard to fiscal matters. Third, real increases in interest rates have also at times tempered the enthusiasm of regions for borrowing. When set against calculations of regional tax resources, the regional debt burden seems easily sustainable (see Table 3:9). In 1992, the ratio of the debt burden (reimbursement in capital + interests) to current resources stood at less than 13 per cent for the regions, compared with 15 per cent for the departments and 19 per cent for the municipalities. Thus, despite the fact that this figure has virtually doubled from 6.6 per cent in 1977, the present level of regional indebtedness is perfectly manageable.

Three general conclusions could be drawn from this overview of the evolution of regional finances since the late 1970s. First, the dramatic increase in regional expenditure and taxes is basically the consequence of massive transfers of responsibilities from the central state to the regions. Even if regional expenditure levels on education or training did explode, no evidence can be found of systematic fiscal waste by the regions. Second, the increase in regional taxes is a direct consequence of the factor just mentioned. It is also a consequence of the inadequate fiscal means transferred to the regions; the subsidies transferred to regions were systematically underestimated and the tax bases transferred were probably too narrow. Third, in such a situation, rational behaviour leads to increased tax rates and heavy borrowing to finance long-term projects, such as education. This is exactly what the French regions did. Moreover, the evolution of fiscal resources over time suggests that French regions have in reality been subject to a severe budgetary constraint. This constraint is partly involuntary – the result of various regulations imposed on regional taxes by the central state and the insufficient nature of subsidies received. In part, however, this constraint is also voluntary. That is, regions are to some extent themselves responsible for determining the levels of regional taxes and borrowing.

WHAT IS THE FUTURE FOR REGIONAL FINANCES?

It is unlikely that French regions are currently so efficient in the provision of regional public goods that we can look forward to large, efficiency surpluses and (by implication) lower taxes. Thus, the future reform of regional taxes remains a key issue for debate. Indeed, this issue has been widely discussed in the recent years (see *Gilbert and Guengant: 1992; Guengant and Uhaldeborde: 1986, 1991*).

With regard to the distribution of resources, two procedures for vertical distribution are conceivable. *Aggregation* (*empilement*) in which either

i) local governments at all levels and the state have the same tax bases and vote for separate rates, or ii) tax revenues are distributed among the fiscal tiers and tax rates are set by the national level (tax sharing). *Specialization* implies the allocation to each local government of a specific array of taxes. No system is perfect. If specialization involves confrontation and conflict over the 'best' allocation of tax bases, aggregation is hardly transparent. Moreover, in both cases, control over all local taxation imposes constraints on the rates. This is a problem which the supporters of specialization deny and those of aggregation fail to address.

International comparisons of local tax systems shed little light on these matters, other than to confirm the limited fiscal powers of regions [*Derycke, 1985; Gilbert and Guengant, 1991*]. The only exception to this general rule is Switzerland (see *Weber* et al., *1992*). Even in Germany the fiscal powers of the German Länder appear to be firmly limited by the Basic Law.

REGIONAL TAX REFORM PROPOSALS

Some proposals simply aim to transfer additional tax bases to the regions. Other, more ambitious proposals seek to address the problem of regional taxation within in the wider framework of a comprehensive tax reform project. Within the first category, it has been proposed that regions should receive part of the revenue from the *Taxe Intérieure sur les Produits Pétroliers* (tax on gasoline), or the revenue from the tax on the land capital gains. Other proposals, such as those put forward by the Guichard Commission in 1986, favoured the introduction of a regional tax on energy usage involving an additional tax on electricity and a new tax on natural gas. A further proposal was that regions should receive part of the revenue accruing to the state from Value Added Tax (TVA) [*Delcamp, 1990*]. However, none of these proposals has been accompanied by convincing arguments with respect to the likely yield, safety, localization, neutrality or even accountability of regional taxes.

More ambitious proposals aim at reforming the system of local taxation as a whole, including regional taxation. Proposals within this category include that put forward by J. P. Fourcade. This recommended that the housing tax (TH) and the two property taxes (TFBNP and TFBP) should remain at the municipal level, while the professional tax (TP) should be restricted to the departments and the regions. A similar project by J. S. Klein seeks to introduce a regional tax on electricity (tax specialization) and a regional tax on 'economic activity' alongside the present system of aggregation at the levels of municipalities and departments. A similar plan put forward by Guengant and Uhaldeborde [*1986*] tends to reinforce the tax specialization among the local governments by separating taxes on inhabitants from taxes on businesses at each level of government. Taxes on inhabitants (TH and TF) would be located at the municipal level; the professional tax (TP) would be levied at the level of urban districts. An explicit linkage between the taxes on inhabitants and those on businesses would, according to this proposal, result from the fiscal exploitation of businesses. At the departmental level there would be a tax on personal income, and at the regional level, a tax on new business creation. The only difficulty, albeit a significant one, with this proposal concerns the problem of decoupling the departmental tax on inhabitants from the regional business tax. A direct interlinking of tax rates between these two tiers is thus unavoidable, which, in turn, necessarily tends to reduce the fiscal autonomy of regions. Reform of regional taxation thus clearly leads to a dilemma. Namely, would it be better to preserve the present system based upon inadequate regional tax bases (too narrow, less bouyant, costly to administer), which nevertheless leaves regions free to determine tax rates? Or would it be better for regions to have adequate tax bases, but less liberty to determine regional tax rates?

THREE POSSIBLE SCENARIOS FOR FRENCH REGIONAL FINANCES

Even if they are not completely realistic, the following three scenarios seek to define the parameters of the debate over how regional finances might be organized in the future.

Preserve the Status Quo *Concerning Regional Functions*

In this situation (implicitly assumed by the majority of regional fiscal reform proposals), competition between the three tiers of local government is likely to result in more regional expenditure and higher regional taxes. This will be necessary to attract population and businesses to the region and to reinforce the strategic position of the regions with respect to the departments. In this situation, it would be difficult to avoid the introduction of additional direct, regional taxes. Any loss in tax receipts would have to be compensated for either by the extension of the regional tax base, or by higher regional tax rates on the present bases.

Enlargement of Regional Responsibilities within a Unitary State

The move towards a two-level organization of the state implies the transfer to the regions of responsibilities currently in the hands of the departments. In such a situation, the problem of the distribution of tax bases becomes easier to solve. The region could either receive exclusively the revenue accruing from a business tax (or from a Value Added Tax – a solution compatible with the current European context) or share with the central state the receipts of a modern, indirect tax (such as gasoline tax – TIPP), or even personal income tax. However, the last case would entail the resolution of complex problems of equalization. A mixed solution is also possible, involving a regional array of taxes including taxes on households and taxes on businesses.

A Regional State

In this highly unlikely scenario, miscellaneous responsibilities presently exerted by the central state would be transferred to the regions which would also receive the corresponding resources. The departmental level once again assumes the usual position of the 'intermediate level' in a three-tiered organization of the state. The transfer of fiscal resources to the regions would need to be very substantial, probably including taxes on businesses. Meanwhile, income tax receipts could be attributed to the department.

CONCLUDING REMARKS

The evolution of regional finances since the 1982 reforms suggests two final remarks and raises two basic issues.

The increase in regional expenditure and regional taxes over the past decade has been quite impressive. The transfer to the regions of responsibilities such as secondary education and training have led to higher public spending and higher taxes. The explanation for such 'overspending' remains unclear. Is it due to the lack of 'accountability' of regional budgets? The result of the inefficiency of particular regional executives and officers? Or, is it simply the expression of voters' preferences for education/training, which have been more closely followed up by the region than they were previously by the central government?

It is clearly important for the central government to control every increase in taxation, given its declared objective of stabilizing the overall tax burden. However, the contribution of regional taxation to the increase of the tax ratio remains limited in importance. Thus regional taxation is not yet a likely threat to French public finances.

The future of regional finances raises various issues. The fiscal *status quo* is likely to lead to more economic inefficiency as the regional tax rates increase. Yet reform of regional taxes is not an easy task. It probably requires a comprehensive reform of the distribution of tax bases among all the levels of government. More 'tax specialization' would probably favour better accountability, but would reduce the liberty of local governments and regions to set tax rates. More tax aggregation (*empilement*) has the (political) merit of maintaining the *status quo*, but would compound the problems of efficiency and accountability.

Finally, the problem of what to do about regional finances raises much wider questions about the territorial organization of the French state. Is a four-level organization sustainable in a unitary state? Does it lead to large efficiency gains or losses? And at what costs? Might it be possible for France to move towards a more federalist (or regionalist) organization of the state? The answers to these questions, are central to the debate on the future of regional finances in France.

REFERENCES

Conseil des Impôts (1989), *10ème Rapport au président de la République relatif à la fiscalité locale* (Paris: Journaux Officiels).

Delcamp, Alain (1990), 'La réforme de la fiscalité régionale' in J.S. Klein (ed.), *Moderniser la fiscalité locale* (Paris: Economica).

Derycke, Pierre-Henri, (1985) 'Les finances des régions - une comparaison internationale', *Revue d'Economie Régionale et Urbaine*, no. 1.

Gilbert, Guy (1991), 'Les ressources financières des Régions', Communication au Colloque O.I.P. 1972-1992 - Deux décennies de régionalisation, Amiens, Octobre.

Gilbert, Guy (1992), 'La spécialisation fiscale verticale', *Revue Française de Finances Publiques*, No. 38, pp.47-55.

Gilbert, Guy, and Alain Guengant (1991), *La fiscalité locale en question* (Paris: Montchrestien).

Guengant, Alain and Jean-Michel Uhaldeborde (1986), 'Crise et réforme de la fiscalité régionale', Communication au 4ème colloque de la Société Française de Finances Publiques, Lyon, mars, miméo.

Hertzog, Robert (1991), 'Les politiques des dépenses des régions', Communication au 4ème Colloque de la Société Française de Finances Publiques, Lyon, mars, miméo.

Labie, François (1991), 'Les politiques fiscales régionales', Communication au 4ème Colloque de la Société Française de Finances Publiques, Lyon, mars, miméo.

Les Notes Bleues (1991), 'Evolution des finances locales et de l'Etat de 1980 à 1990', No. 561, 3-13 octobre.

Marchand, Marie-Jacqueline (1987a), 'L'impact financier de la décentralisation. Le cas de la formation professionnelle' in G.R.A.L. *Annuaire des Collectivités Locales* (Paris: LITEC), pp.37-47.

Marchand, Marie-Jacqueline (1987b), 'La décentralisation: les budgets régionaux entre l'ajustement et la traverse', *Revue Française d'Economie Régionale et Urbaine*, No. 4, pp.531-553.

Marchand, Marie-Jacqueline (1991), 'Les lycées, les régions: An III', *Politique et Management Public*, Vol. 9, No. 1, pp.47-66

From Regional to Sectoral Policies: The Contractual Relations Between the State and the Regions in France

RICHARD BALME and LAURENCE BONNET

INTRODUCTION

The 1982 decentralization reforms significantly changed the territorial organization of the French state. The reforms also changed the nature of the relationship between the state and local or intermediate governments. The reforms restructured cooperation arrangements between the state and regional/local authorities and readjusted their respective contributions to sectoral policies. This created a new style of territorial politics. The expansion of contractual planning after 1982 has been central to this process. Planning contracts established through a bargaining process between the state and the regions (*Contrats de Plan Etat-Régions*) aim to define common objectives and secure financial cooperation on a pluri-annual basis. *Contrats de Plan* are now the major institutional mechanism responsible for organizing centre-periphery relations in the realm of public policy. As such, they can be viewed as a crucial indicator of the new pattern of territorial integration generated by the French decentralization reforms.

The use of contractual agreements between the state and local governments predates the Defferre reforms. Since the 1970s, agreements of this type have existed between national governments and urban districts (*communautés urbaines*), medium-sized cities and rural areas (*contrats villes moyennes* and *contrats de pays*). They were initiated by national governments anxious to improve sectoral policy coordination and ensure the compatibility of state and local authority investment. At the regional level, contractual arrangements were first introduced following the regionalization of the VIIth and VIIIth Plans in the form of *Programmes d'Action Prioritaire d'Initiative Régionale* [*De Lanversin* et al., *1989*]. Undoubtedly, contractual planning is rooted in the origins of the French region conceived as a functional tool for structural and regional planning [*Quermonne, 1963*]. However, before the decentralization reforms of the 1980s, the regions could hardly enter into a real contractual relationship with the state as their resources remained limited, and above all their chief executive was the regional prefect.[1] With the law of 29 March 1982, regions became formally responsible for regional economic development and were accorded the necessary legal status to negotiate with state representatives. The French planning reform, adopted on 29 July 1982, asserted that the vocation of the region was to elaborate regional plans, to contribute to the preparation of the national plan and to participate in its implementation through *contrats de plan*. The rules organizing these contracts were subsequently specified by ordinance on 21 January 1983. The first two generations of these contracts covered the periods 1984-1988 and 1989-1993. The third generation was adopted in early 1994.

Contractual relations are driven by three different forces and bring together personnel from three distinct policy sectors: the tradition of French national planning, conducted since 1946 by the *Commissariat Général du Plan* (CGP); regional policy conducted since 1963 by the *Délégation à l'Aménagement du Territoire et à l'Action Régionale* (DATAR); and the decentralization reforms elaborated since 1982 by the Ministry of Interior. In more analytical terms, planning contracts are a product of complex influences - of 'macro' versus 'micro' types of policy (national planning versus regional policy) and of sectoral versus institutional types of policy (regional policy versus decentralization). They appear as a genuine instrument to manage centre-periphery relations and, possibly, to articulate the different objectives and characteristics of these three policy areas.

The argument presented below is that just like the decentralization reforms generally, contractual relations have, for political and organizational reasons, been dominated by ambiguous objectives, implementation problems and lack of clarity. Thus, whilst regions now have some room for manoeuvre, the state retains much influence. Nevertheless, the institutionalization of negotiations and the introduction of regional political autonomy is a major shift and is crucial in organizing the new, bargaining style of relations between regions and the state. The dominant characteristics of planning contracts have also become more distinctive; they have become more 'micro' than 'macro' and more institutional than sectoral in nature. Thus, it can be argued that contractualization is indeed a new policy style, distinguishable from both centralized planning and traditional regional policy. As such *contrats de plan* constitute a new institutional mechanism designed to ensure cooperation between actors in a post-unitary state. We will first analyze the procedures associated with the formulation of contractual plans before considering the implications of their implementation for the territorial policy-making process.

THE CHRONOLOGICAL DEVELOPMENT OF INTERGOVERNMENTAL RELATIONS

To be properly understood, the contractual relations between the state and the regions have first to be approached through a chronological perspective.

The institutional technique of contractualization was initially conceived by the DATAR. However, the reality of this new policy-making process was shaped and adapted over time by both top-down and bottom-up pressures. Changing political circumstances also prompted changes in the objectives and functions assigned to contractualization. Finally, the bargaining processes introduced with this kind of planning necessarily occurs over a rather protracted period of time. Bureaucrats and political leaders spontaneously refer in interviews to dates, rounds and deadlines, as the first evidence of contractual relations. In this area maybe more than in others, the political agenda is sequential rather than synchronic or static. Appreciation of the dynamics of contractual relations is essential to their understanding, and we must therefore begin with an examination of the different steps and the different moves involved in this process.

Decentralizing the National Plan

The contractual policy-making process started in July 1982 when regions were asked to list their regional investment priorities [*Carsalade, 1989*]. These objectives were to be taken into account in the formulation of the IXth national plan for the 1984-1989 period. Regional planning priorities which were likely to be included in planning contracts were then identified by regional prefects, following discussions with regional councils. These regional proposals, specified without any reference to national planning objectives, were thereafter scrutinized and considered by the different central administrations involved in the preparation of the national plan. The resulting decisions were confirmed during a meeting of the interministerial committee in charge for regional planning (*Comité Interministériel à l'Aménagement du Territoire - CIAT*) in April 1983. The major policy areas selected for contractualization were employment, vocational training, development of new technologies, support to export business, development of services for small and medium-sized regional firms, diversification of agricultural production, support to craft industry, better use of energy, and environmental protection. At the same time, prefects were asked to pay attention to national priorities defined by the bill of 18 April 1983 when discussing with the regional executives pilot studies prefiguring contractual plans. After a first assessment, both the purpose and the scope of the contracts were specified following an appraisal of the pilot studies by the CIAT on 27 July 1983. Finally, directions were conveyed by state representatives to regional executives in order for contracts to be drawn up. Draft contracts were sent to the Secretary of State in charge of the plan in November 1983, and then finalized during a CIAT meeting in December 1983. In anticipation of further requests being submitted by some regions, provision was made for reexamination of the contract proposals by the CIAT in April 1984. In the event, arbitration was required for 12 regions. Despite the short time periods allowed for the elaboration of both regional plans and the corresponding contracts, the entire exercise was completed on time: 21 metropolitan regions out of 22 signed their *contrats de plan* between March and July 1984. The plan for Corsica was not signed until May 1985 because of the political troubles encountered by the first elected regional assembly, which was dissolved on June 1984. Generally speaking, the first generation of planning contracts established a number of lasting features of the contract-making process: a continuous flow of relations between centre and periphery through permanent administrative procedures of bargaining; interaction between central and regional levels in defining the areas suitable for contractualization; and the rather loose coherence of territorial policy – torn between the macro-level of national planning and the micro-level of regional policy.

Focusing Objectives in the Second Generation

In April 1987, the CIAT announced that planning contracts would be used for the 1989-1993 national plan. However, the process was to be refined in three ways. First, the new contracts were to be more selective. In particular, they were to correspond with strategic development programmes conceived within a European perspective. Second, the procedures involved were to be simplified. More specifically, contracts were to be self-sufficient – that is, would not require further sub-contracts for their implementation, as had frequently occurred in the previous period. Finally, the role of the regional prefects in the negotiation process was to be strengthened.

Regional prefects and presidents of regional councils were consulted about their mid-term priorities during the fall of 1987. As reported by the DATAR, three main types of concern emerged: the improvement of communication infrastructure and particularly roads; the increase of training and research capacities; and the need to conduct development policies relating to specific regional situations. Four areas were then opened to contractualization in February 1988: infrastructure; education and training; support to research programmes and development of technology; local development programmes based on concertation (*Programmes d'Aménage-ment Concerté du Territoire* – PACT). On assuming office in 1988, the Socialist government of Prime Minister Michel Rocard expressed great interest in contractual plans, the content of which was further defined by an interministerial meeting in August 1988, chaired by the Prime Minister. On the one hand, stress was placed on actions contributing to local economic development and employment. This objective was formalized in the creation of a special fund (*Fond Régionalisé d'Aide aux Initiatives Locales* – FRILE), of FF250 million to finance appropriate projects within planning contracts. On the other hand, contractualization was used to reinforce urban social policies such as urban PACT and community development programmes (*Développement Social des Quartiers* – DSQ). Moreover, regions were asked to identify clearly and map the areas where PACT, particularly rural ones, were going to be implemented. Thus, while the objectives of the planning contracts became more focused, the scope of contractualization was also reduced, compared with that of the IXth Plan.

The next step in the elaboration of the 1989-93 planning contracts was taken in November 1988 when the CIAT took receipt of drafts and determined the global amount of state credits. The process was ultimately closed by two further CIAT meetings in February 1989: the signature of 15 contracts already adopted by regional councils was authorized while the signature of six others was allowed, subject to their being approved by regional councils. Finalization of the Ile-de-France contract took rather longer – it was finally signed in May 1989. Every metropolitan *contrat de plan* had been signed between February and May 1989. As with the IXth Plan, the DATAR was in charge of the intergovernmental coordination of the procedure, keeping in continuous touch with prefects.

Several features of this intergovernmental policy process are revealed by this brief historical account. First, contractual planning appears as a social construction of time, anticipating the future and reducing uncertainty, securing the consistency of public policies through the commitment of participants. The contract effectively defines a period during which cooperation is secured by the agreement. This is clearly crucial in securing relative stability of public intervention and its maintenance over time. The contract is also defined by a deadline at which point in time it will be renewed, thereby implying a conscious re-examination of objectives and mutual adaptation of behaviour. In other words, planning contracts are binding, but for a limited time at the end of which participants have to renegotiate the terms of their cooperation. This helps to make the regional institution part of this relationship, as a player using self-presentation techniques and strategic moves in a bargaining process. This social construction of time is also an administrative phenomenon. Indeed the periodization introduced by the contractual process is a powerful tool with which to organize a cognitive representation of public policy for participants and to coordinate their formal tasks. In other words, the sequential dimension of the planning process has been essential in defining a new division of labour in the political and administrative spheres concerned with territorial management.

From a more empirical perspective, the formulation of contractual relations involves a continuous exchange of information and bargaining between the centre and the periphery. This places prefects in a key position within the planning process. They act as *missi dominici*, expressing the voice of the state within regions, they prepare the regional plans, and they act as policy brokers in the very early stages of policy formulation. Their role is further enhanced by the fact that *contrats de plan* cover two distinct policy areas: economic and structural planning (*planification*) – at least for the first generation – and regional policy (*aménagement du territoire*). Objectives of the national plans are defined by the CGP (under the direct authority of the Prime Minister), whereas *contrats de plan* are prepared under the leadership of the DATAR (under the authority of the ministry of territorial planning (*Aménagement du Territoire*) before being adopted by the CIAT. Inter-organizational relations, both vertical between different levels of government, and horizontal between different policy areas and administrations, have thus necessarily become more important and increasingly formalized. They have also become more autonomous, as exemplified by the progressive divergence between national and contractual planning. Despite the concentration of planning objectives in the second generation, contractual plans between regions and the state were signed before the Xth national plan was adopted in July 1989. The national plan follows and in a way reflects the contractual agreements between the state and the regions. However, the organizational design of the policy reflects an ambiguity of goals which will become more salient in the following sections.

'SECTORALIZATION' OF CONTRACTUAL PLANNING

The contractual planning process appears as both a transfer of resources from the state to the regions and the mobilization of local capacities to sustain sectoral policies concerning the national territory as a whole. The policy is therefore both hierarchical, with regard to the redistribution of resources across the territory, and cooperative in its allocative aspect. From an analytical point of view, two major difficulties arise. First, there is an apparent contradiction between redistribution – that is, the reduction of regional inequalities requiring state intervention – and decentralization, which is a cooperative mode of policy-making allowing competition and therefore inequalities between regions. Second, it is difficult to evaluate the redistributive impact of contractual planning. Poorer regions do receive comparatively more in state transfers than richer ones (in per capita terms). But how should we measure the redistributive impact of these differences? In terms of policy intentions (that is, measuring the relative importance of state subsidies to regions), or in terms of effective impact (that is, measuring the economic impact of regional *contrats de plan*)? If the latter, at what stage in the implementation process should evaluation take place? We must also remember that even when regional disparities persist, public policy may play an important role in preventing or limiting a worsening situation. Any attempt to measure the impact of contractual plans is further complicated by the fact that these are by no means the only transfer of resources from the centre to the periphery. The financial aspect of contractual relations has therefore to be approached cautiously by political analysts. Some major trends can nevertheless be identified from a longitudinal examination of the respective contributions of the state and the regions to the plans, and comparison of the sectoral and regional distribution of funds. This analysis suggests that there has been no clearly defined policy objective behind the contractualization process; rather the planning contracts were shaped by mixed and somewhat ambiguous policy aims.

Distributive Policy from the Centre to the Periphery

In the first generation of *contrats de plan*, global credits amounted to FF73 billion, with overseas regions receiving FF3.4 billion (see Table 4:1). In global terms the ratio of state to metropolitan regional contribution was 1:5.[2] At this stage, contractual planning may therefore be described as a redistributive policy from the state to the regions rather than the mobilization of peripheral resources. However, this state-region financial participation ratio varied quite significantly between regions from 0.8 in Ile-de-France, to 2.9 in Languedoc-Roussillon and 8.3 in French Guiana. Generally speaking, the relative importance of the state's contribution was greater in peripheral regions than in others (3.2 in overseas regions compared with 1.5 in the metropolitan ones) reflecting the regional policy dimension of *contrats de plan*, which sought to reduce regional disparities. This objective is also evident in the distribution of funds between policy areas and the priority given to transportation (38 per cent), before economic development (17 per cent), health care and social policy (11 per cent); vocational training (10 per cent); environment (eight per cent); leisure, culture, tourism and sport (six per cent); research and technological development (three per cent).

Though the planning procedure aims to reduce regional disparities, the spatial distribution of population concentrates regional problems as well as fiscal capacities. In consequence, large regions such as Ile-de-France, Nord-Pas-de-Calais, Rhône-Alpes and Provence-Alpes-Côte d'Azur received 47.9 per cent of the total state contribution for 1984-88. Powerful, prosperous and heavily populated regions thus received an important proportion of state aid. Viewed from this perspective, structural planning seems to have been more

TABLE 4:1
CONTRATS DE PLAN ETAT-REGION 1984-1988
VOLUME OF STATE AND REGIONS' CONTRIBUTIONS
(MILLIONS FRANCS)

Region	(1)	(2)	(3)	(4)
	State	**Region**	**Total**	**(1)/(2)**
Alsace	1,117	719	1,836	1.6
Aquitaine	2,138	1,333	3,471	1.6
Auvergne	980	534	1,514	1.8
Bourgogne	945	640	1,585	1.5
Bretagne	1,949	978	2,927	2.0
Centre	840	580	1,420	1.4
Champagne-Ardennes	595	455	1,050	1.3
Corse	850	360	1,210	2.4
Franche-Comté	917	568	1,458	1.6
Ile-de-France	7,238	8,562	15,800	0.8
Languedoc-Roussillon	2,073	850	2,923	2.4
Limousin	721	316	1,037	2.3
Lorraine	3,058	1,049	4,107	2.9
Midi-Pyrenées	1,615	827	2,422	2.0
Nord-Pas-de-Calais	4,472	2,462	6,934	1.8
Basse-Normandie	779	487	1,266	1.6
Haute-Normandie	509	523	1,032	1.0
Pays de Loire	1,405	985	2,390	1.4
Picardi	1,949	1,025	2,974	1.9
Poitou--Charentes	1,050	567	1,617	1.9
Provence-Alpes-Cote-d'Azur	4,137	2,664	6,801	1.6
Rhône-Alpes	2,533	1,516	4,049	1.7
Total Metropole	**41,870**	**28,000**	**69,870**	**1.5**
Guadeloupe	613	247	860	2.5
Guyane	679	81	760	8.3
Martinique	492	144	636	3.4
Réunion	823	330	1,153	2.5
Total DOM	2,607	802	3,409	3.2
Total Metropole + DOM	44,477	28,802	73,279	1.5

Source: Commissariat Général au Plan.

important as a policy objective than the reduction of regional disparities.
(see Table 4:2). Globally, regions devoted just over a quarter of their budgets
to planning contracts (26 per cent for the metropolitan regions in 1986). The
proportion ranged from 39.1 per cent for Ile-de-France to 13.3 per cent for
Limousin, with Provence-Alpes-Côtes d'Azur and Nord-Pas-de-Calais
allocating 28 per cent and 27 per cent of their budgets respectively to
contrats de plan (*Conseil économique et social*, 1989). This gives a measure
of the importance of intergovernmental relations in the territorial policy
process, at least from the regional point of view. The first generation of
contracts presents a picture of a joint policy process, and the use of state

TABLE 4:2
CONTRATS DE PLAN ETAT-REGION 1984-1988
STATE AND REGIONS' CONTRIBUTION (%)

Region	State	Region	Total
Alsace	2.5	2.5	2.5
Aquitaine	4.8	4.6	4.7
Auvergne	2.2	1.9	2.1
Bourgogne	2.1	2.2	2.2
Bretgne	4.4	3.4	4.0
Centre	1.9	2.0	1.9
Champagne-Ardennes	1.3	1.6	1.4
Corse	1.9	1.2	1.7
Franche-Comté	2.1	2.0	2.0
Ile-de-France	16.3	29.7	21.6
Languedoc-Roussillon	4.6	3.0	4.0
Limousin	1.6	1.1	1.4
Lorrraine	6.9	3.6	5.6
Mid-Pyrénées	3.6	2.9	3.3
Nord-Pad-de-Calais	10.1	8.5	9.5
Basse-Normandie	1.8	1.7	1.7
Haute-Normandie	1.1	1.8	1.4
Pays de Loire	3.1	3.4	3.3
Picardie	4.4	3.5	4.0
Poitou-Charentes	2.4	2.0	2.2
Provence-Alpes-Côte-d'Azur	9.3	9.3	9.3
Rhône-Alpes	5.7	5.3	5.5
Total Metropole	94.1	97.2	95.3
Guadeloupe	1.4	0.9	1.2
Guyane	1.5	0.3	1.0
Martinique	1.1	0.5	0.9
Reunion	1.9	1.1	1.6
Total DOM	5.9	2.8	4.7
Total Metropole + DOM	100.0	100.0	100.0

Source: Commissariat Général au Plan.

resources to encourage the development of regional policies. The policy which emerged from this process represented the aggregation of decentralized bargaining within the boundaries of a financial package defined by the state.

From Territorial to Sectoral Policies

The state planned to allocate some FF52 billion to the second generation of *contrats de plan*. The credits were divided up as follows: FF23.3 billion for infrastructural development; FF12 billion for the PACT; FF8.7 billion for training and research; and FF8.1 billion for employment and economic development. Following the rationale imposed by the growth of their own development policies, some regions asked for specific state interventions such as the Cross-Channel Programme, to be listed in *contrats de plan* in order to give greater visibility to their actions. With these additional credits, the global share of the state amounted to FF54.9 billions (see Table 4:3). In comparison with the IXth plan, state credits increased by 25 per cent (in current values) and the scope of contractualization narrowed. More resources were therefore allocated to the implementation of fewer policies, defined as priorities. The financial involvement of regions in the second planning exercise totalled FF43 billion (compared with FF28 billion for the IXth plan). Their overall contribution amounted to 45 per cent of total expenditure, compared with 40 per cent for the IXth plan. If we include the additional contributions of towns and departments to the programmes, more than FF100 billion were allocated to these contracts. In comparison with the

TABLE 4:3
CONTRATS DE PLAN ETAT-REGION 1989-1993
PROGRAMMED EXPENDITURE AS REPORTED BY REGIONAL PREFECTS
(MILLIONS FRANCS)

	STATE	REGIONS
Regions	Affichage global Etat	Affichage intervention des conseils régionaux
Alsace	1,688.659	2,085.16
Aquitaine	2,151.75	1,528.52
Auvergne	1,356.30	701.45
Bourgogne	1,550.12	1,002.90
Bretagne	3,637.80	1,873.60
Centre	1,578.55	1,092.11
Champagne	1,333.82	1,312.02
Corse	517.07	324.79
Franche-Comté	1,357.80	862.07
Ile-de-France	8,522.00	14,460.00
Languedoc-Roussillon	2,606.67	1,415.25
Limousin	1,129.29	644.59
Lorraine	3,254.83	1,908.09
Mid-Pyrénées	3,355.00	1,661.00
Nord-Pas-de-Calais	5,330.90	3,470.27
Basse-Normandie	1,654.50	1,298.33
Haute-Normandie	1,453.32	1,323.82
Pays de Loire	1,995.87	1,404.12
Picardie	2,131.90	1,442.84
Poitou-Charentes	1,697.91	1,257.20
Provence-Alpes-Côtes-d'Azur	2,860.00	2,326.00
Rhône-Alpes	3,8087.00	2,590.70
Total France	**54,971.09**	**45,984.83**

Source: DATAR.

previous period, the ratio appears more favourable towards the state, with regions contributing more in both absolute and relative terms. The average state-region participation ratio was 1.19, ranging from 0.58 in Ile-de-France to 2.14 in Midi-Pyrénées. The second generation of contracts clearly involved an increased mobilization of regional resources within the joint policy process.

The 1989-1993 *contrats de plan* were presented as a favoured tool for regional development policy for four reasons [*Lehericy, 1989*]. First, it was argued that contractualization makes easier the concentration of credits on sectoral priorities. The content of the new contracts was intended to fit more explicitly the goals of both partners and to be more directly related to a European framework for regional policies. Second, it was claimed that the procedures involved (especially PACT) provided an incentive for regions to define infra-regional areas for priority funding. The spatial definition of programmes could in this way be fine-tuned. Third, *contrats de plan* were also conceived as a flexible territorial policy tool which permitted the government and regions to respond financially to changing priorities. This belief is reflected in sectors such as training, research, roads and PACT, where contracts are important in the budgetary planning of sectoral policies and the definition of their territorial implementation. Finally, the regional share-out of state credits was intended to emphasize the redistributive aspect of the policy. For instance, Corsica received FF2,100 per capita and Limousin FF1,453, compared with a national average of FF930 per capita.

Nevertheless, such a concentration of objectives induced a greater selectivity of projects, which from the viewpoint of regions meant increased pressure from the state. In practice, regions have not played the leading role formally ascribed to them by contractual planning procedures, especially in the case of the Xth Plan. The greater focusing of objectives introduced in 1988 by the Socialist government of Michel Rocard (former Minister for Planning 1981-83) was intended to avoid the dispersal of credits and the somewhat uncoordinated outcomes of the bargaining process. Yet, the need for the regions to be more selective when submitting proposals for joint financing necessarily led them to include actions which they knew to be compatible with national sectoral priorities. Consequently, a reversal of initiative occurred in the policy-making process with regional plans becoming the result of the contractualization process rather than its guiding principle. With the concentration of objectives, the rationale for contrac-tualization became more sectoral than territorial: contractual plans therefore now seem to be more a technique to ensure the territorial coordination of unemployment or urban policy, for example, than a specific tool to reduce regional disparities. Regions thus had to face both the relative retreat of the state financially and the greater selectivity of central government support for their policies. Moreover, sectorization of planning contracts further reduced the capacity of regions to target more effectively their interventions. Compared with the preparation of the IXth plan, regions were more involved in the formulation of the Xth plan, albeit with less ability to define its scope and objectives. Notwithstanding some redistributive efforts, contractualization now appears more as the partial regionalization of sectoral policies under the control of the state than as the cooperative management of a redistributive, regional policy.

THE POLITICAL TRANSFORMATION OF THE REGIONAL TERRITORY

The implementation of contractual planning also prompted a transformation of relations between political, bureaucratic and private policy actors at the regional level. This transformation was highly complex in nature due to the diversity of sectoral policies and interests affected, the overlap of three different tiers of local government, the fragmented nature of the state administration, and regional variations in socio-economic and/or cultural characteristics. Moreover, the specific impact of contractual plans within the decentralization programme as a whole is difficult to separate from other changes. Nevertheless, some conclusions can be drawn from a series of evaluation studies conducted by the *Commissariat Général du Plan*, and more recently by research undertaken by the *Conseil Economique et Social* and a joint working group from the CGP and the DATAR [*Commissariat Général du Plan, 1985; Conseil Economique et Social, 1991; Commissariat Général du Plan, Délégation à l'Aménagement du Territoire et à l'Action Régionale, 1991*]. These studies revealed some common tendencies and identified several problems the third generation of contracts would have to tackle.

The Lack of Political Consistency of the Regional Territory

The weakness of concertation between various policy actors within the region and the potential tensions between the region and other levels of territorial government prompted questions about the role of the region within the planning process. Consultation with cities, departments and other local bodies (public and private), formally required in the preparation of regional *contrats de plan*, was in practice extremely variable both in type and degree. Consultation with sectoral interests tended to be conducted via the *Conseil Economique et Social Régional* – CESR – a consultative body, representing the major socio-economic interests within the region. In some regions the CESR was directly involved in the formulation of the regional plan, whilst in others it was consulted much later and had little or no opportunity to amend the project. Large firms, despite their impact on employment and economic development, tended not to become involved in the process. Actions listed in contractual plans were not directly relevant to them and they tended instead to be more interested in the development of national and international level economic strategies. In short, there is a tension between the needs of planners and those of private firms: economic planning necessarily imposes some constraints and obligations upon companies, who would prefer not to have to consider the social and territorial impact of their investment decisions. Evidence suggests that the regional policy impact of contractual planning was limited by the fact that large firms were able to avoid making any territorial commitments.

The law obliged the regions to consult constituent departments, major cities and towns with a population over 10,000, but left the means of doing this to their own discretion. In practice, local political circumstances determined the form taken by this consultation. However, departments were reluctant to allow regions to take the lead in operations requiring departments to make a financial contribution, for example in road construction. Simultaneous implementation of the decentralization programme and contractual plans created new tensions in the relationships between regions and other local authorities. For example, the state and the regions signed planning contracts covering a range of tasks, responsibility for which was then handed over to the departments and communes (as part of the decentralization process). Additionally, programme contracts with other local authorities were therefore required for the implementation of contractual plans. Predictably, there were also tensions between regions and constituent authorities over the financing of planning contracts. Where *contrats de plan* provided financial support to departments and communes, assessments were often carried out by commissions composed mainly of state and regional representatives. This practice was denounced by some recipient local authorities as a new form of financial *'tutelle'*. Other departments complained that they were only invited to participate in the contractualization process because of their financial capacities. Moreover, departments and communes also complained that regions frequently committed local authorities to projects without any prior consultation. Indeed, as confirmed by the evaluation studies listed above, *concertation* between regions and local authorities was either non-existent or very formal, underlining the fact that regions could not or did not want to play the role of a 'unifier' for regional development. This reluctance can be explained by two sets of reasons. First, the consultation procedures were extremely bureaucratic and complex in nature. Several rounds of bargaining between regions and prefects and between regions and central administrative agencies took place within a short timetable set by the government. This schedule imposed considerable pressures upon regions, who lacked the necessary expertise, resources and administrative personnel to conduct adequate consultations in the time available. Second, regions are still immature institutions compared with cities or departments and lack the political and legal authority to negotiate effectively with other local governments in situations of conflict. The weakness of *concertation* in the contractualization process can, in some cases, also be understood as a deliberate strategy designed to enhance the status and influence of regional political leaders within the process. This strategy served merely to exacerbate tensions between regional and local political leaders and was dysfunctional to the planning exercise.

Not surprisingly, implementation difficulties were greatest in those regions where departments were only very loosely involved in the working out of contracts. Departments have since requested that the contractualization procedure be formally extended so as to result in state-region-department contracts. Indeed, when preparing the third generation of contracts (1994-1998), the government did consider the possibility of entering into contracts with departments as well as with regions. Though the idea was eventually abandoned, it nevertheless provided an incentive for regions to build a better partnership with the other levels of local government. Municipalities, who regarded themselves as having been relatively unaffected by the earlier planning contracts, save for a few specific types of action (such as the *Développement Social des Quartiers* programme) also demanded a bigger say in the preparation of the third generation of contracts. With both departments and municipalities now pressing to play a more active role in the planning process, the policy-making role of the region has become weaker. Indeed, regions have become centres for the coordination of multiple actors and initiatives rather than institutions capable of imposing their own political will upon the territory. This development is not surprising given that the capacity of regions to mobilize support from infra-regional governments is administratively and legally weak and highly dependent upon political resources. The institutional and political fragmentation of the regional territory has thus imposed important constraints upon the contractual planning process.

Calling for Déconcentration

All evaluations of the contractualization process agreed upon the need for further administrative *déconcentration* to improve the planning process. In particular, it was recommended that the prefect should play a more important role in the planning process to become the principal negotiator and coordinator of the *contrats de plan*. Moreover, it was proposed that this increased power of decision-making should be enjoyed throughout the entire process, from the determination of the national planning priorities by the state to supervision of the implementation of contracts. Prefects were thus mandated to negotiate the third round of planning contracts. However, administrative *déconcentration* has been opposed in various quarters. The finance ministry, for example, is not in favour of contractual planning and has frozen a number of state credits, thereby limiting the options open to prefects. Nor is it willing to allow 22 regional prefectures to have at their disposal non-allocated state credits in a period of budget restrictions. Moreover, this reluctance is shared by a number of technical and departmental administrations (for example, agriculture, roads and infrastructure). In order to protect their status within the politico-administrative hierarchy, central sectoral administrations have opposed the development of close relationships between prefects and their respective field services. In order to preserve their financial autonomy, departmental administrations have generally shunned contractualization, except in those instances where it can be used as a means of extracting additional resources from the Ministry of Finance. Contractual planning clearly strengthens the public administrations of the central government departments at the regional level around prefects. However, the key *regional* actors in this process – the prefect and the president of the regional council – are caught up in a much bigger, *national* power struggle, which in turn has important implications for the region.

THE CRISIS OF CONTRACTUAL POLICY-MAKING?

Notwithstanding the innovations which have been introduced in the territorial policy-making process, contractual relations between the state and the regions remain rather tenuous. Contracts have been progressively disconnected from strategic, regional policies with the decline of national planning and the difficulties associated with regional planning. The absence of any regional level of evaluation of contractualization has left regions unable to see how and why the process might be improved. Finally, some important tensions can be detected in the negotiations for the current generation of contracts for 1994-1998.

The Autonomy of Contractualization within the Policy Process

A major problem associated with the experience of the *contrats de plan* is the progressive 'autonomization' of contracts with regard to national and infra-regional planning strategies [*Madiot, 1989*]. Analysis of the content of the first contracts shows that most of the actions were compatible with the objectives of the IXth plan. Achieving this 'fit' was not, however, a simple task. The regional planning procedures had to be brought forward in order that regional requests for assistance could be included in the preparation of the state budget. Therefore, the state relied upon the regional prefects to identify the actions to be listed in contractual plans before the regional councils had finished their own work. As a result, the central government's own objectives tended to prevail in the *contrats de plan*, except in those regions which managed to meet the earlier deadline. Furthermore, as indicated above, the procedures encouraged regions to adjust their own priorities to coincide with the national ones in order to secure more state credits.

The contractualization process has become progressively detached from national and infra-regional level planning. When the decision was taken to maintain contractual planning for the 1989-1993 Xth plan, the government decided to dissociate it from the national planning process, ostensibly because the latter was to be delayed by the 1988 legislative elections. Contractual plans were thus no longer to be mechanisms for the implementation and coordination of regional and national plans. They became instead a means of establishing institutional linkages between the state and regions to enforce decentralization. More specifically, they were intended to induce and manage the controlled regionalization of sectoral policies. Thus, in most regions, problems caused by the non-existence or weakness of regional plans was compounded by the lack of a national plan underpinning the 1989-1993 generation of contracts. The tenuous revival of national planning when the socialists came back into office in 1988 prompted a re-evaluation of the link between contractual plans and the national plan. Assessments of both the first and second generation of planning contracts clearly highlighted the extent to which these had become 'free-floating' entities: only five regions had prepared detailed regional plans for the first planning period (1984-1988) rising to 14 for the second period (1989-1993). Such a progression is in part due to pressure from the European Union: regions applying for EU structural funds must submit a strategic regional development plan to the European Commission (see chapter by Sonia Mazey in this volume). The persistent failure of several regions to produce a strategic development plan (as legally required by the 1982 decentralization reforms) constitutes a further example of the incremental adaptation of these reforms in practice. In similar vein, the second generation of contracts were signed before the objectives of the national plan were even determined. As regards the third generation (1994-1998), contracts were negotiated in early 1994; only afterwards were regions consulted over the national plan. Thus, part of the decentralized planning law of July 1982, has fallen into abeyance, whilst national planning has declined to the point where it involves little more than formal consultation with the regions and no binding commitments. The fact that the national plan covers a four year period and *contrats de plan* span a five year period further reinforces the independent nature of the latter. In such a context, contractual plans have tended to assume their own rationale – contracts without plans. Two additional developments have served to undermine further the status of contractual planning. First, competing policies have emerged which by-pass the contractualization process [*Moreau, 1989*]. Second, the growth of contractual arrangements especially in the field of urban policies, has resulted in the emergence of significant – and unpopular – regional disparities in the provision of public services.

   In one sense, the progressive separation of contractualization from the planning process is an indicator of the degree to which they have become institutionalized. Whether or not contractual planning constitutes an effective regional policy instrument (nationally or regionally defined) remains open to question. Yet, regional policy is by no means the only rationale for contractualization. Contracts may well prove a successful means of funding and managing regionalized sectoral policies under state control.

How to Evaluate the Policy Process?

Given the inadequacy of comparative financial data relating to the implementation of *contrats de plan*, it is difficult to evaluate their real impact. A major reason for the paucity of information is the lack of uniformity in the presentation of regional accounts. Regional variations in documentation are to some extent a function of the complex budgetary procedures involved. First, some 18 months may elapse between the allocation of a credit and the record of its expenditure, because of the time required to draw up the balance-sheet. Second, it is often difficult to identify partners other than the state and the regions, not least because local authority accounts are often difficult to interpret. Third, the total amount of money allocated to programmes is not always listed in *contrats de plan* except for road programmes. For example, whether or not the credits listed are inclusive of tax or not is not always specified, yet VAT represents a difference of some FF20 billion for the second generation of *contrats de plan*. Central government budgetary regulations further complicate the assessment of the contractualization process. Financial commitments entered into by the state are subject to the programme authorization rule. This means that there is a two-year delay between the authorization of the credit and full payment of it. Thus, the total time required for the financing of *contrats de plan* is seven years bearing in mind the state budgetary rules.

Finally, the interministerial body set up on 22 January 1990 for public policy evaluation is concerned only with the activities of national public policies. As such, it does not evaluate local authority actions based upon contracts involving the state. These methodological difficulties have limited meaningful evaluation of the *contrats de plan*. This is not merely an academic problem: the absence of evaluation procedures threatens the legitimacy of the process. Not surprisingly, potential signatories feel uneasy about committing themselves financially to contracts which lack financial transparency and which cannot be easily monitored during and after implementation.

The Third Generation of Contrats de Plan

The shift towards a greater selectivity in the determination of objectives was confirmed by negotiations surrounding the most recent generation of *contrats de plan*. As the press release of the CIAT issued on 23 July 1992 stated, the participants should 'concentrate the contractualization field on geographical or economic areas having priority, so as to make the contracts more consistent with future European assistance programmes directed towards regions with structural handicaps'. This position was confirmed by the new government of Edouard Balladur, elected in March 1993. Prefects were asked to negotiate with regions according to a rationale that was 'geographical and no longer sectoral'. The volume and regional distribution of the state contribution was decided during a CIAT meeting held on 12 July 1993. Symbolically, this was held in Mende, a small town of the rural Lozère department in order to demonstrate the political commitment of the government to the development of truly regional policies. The government announced a contribution of FF83.5 billion to be allocated in variable proportions, depending on the economic wealth of regions. Regional councils protested vigorously against both the low level of state participation and the criteria used to determine the distribution of this sum. In the event, some regions obtained additional credits. Nevertheless the negotiations were marked by severe conflict. Delays occurred as revision of the state proposals was required in most cases. In November 1993, Limousin broke off negotiations with the state for a period of three weeks, and in January 1994 Haute-Normandie rejected the *contrat de plan* apparently definitively. Several other regions including Aquitaine, Poitou-Charentes, Pays-de-la-Loire and Centre, threatened not to sign a contract. Regional discontent centres upon the low level of state participation and the apparent reluctance of the state to comply with procedures. Specific complaints include the fact that the scope for contractualization is not negotiable and includes areas which lie beyond the policy competence of regions, such as education (*programme université 2000*) or urban planning (*contrats de ville*). Moreover, it appears that the government took a number of decisions unilaterally at the Mende meeting regarding the allocation of a 'hard core' (that is, 60 per cent) of its contribution. Regional leaders talk of a 'sophisticated technique' designed to devolve the financial costs of state responsibilities and some even doubt that the procedure could be used again in the future. Admittedly, some attempts have been made to tackle previous difficulties. These include the introduction of evaluation measures at the regional level and the greater emphasis upon the spatial rather than the sectoral dimension of contracts. Nevertheless, for the reasons outlined above, the contractualization process, as originally envisaged, is now in crisis and rapidly losing legitimacy among participants. Though crucial for the regions, the credits allocated to contractualization by the state now constitute only a small part of its expenditure within the region. Moreover, the current contractual planning process is, despite government reassurances to the contrary, totally disconnected from the recent attempt to revive territorial policy of *aménagement du territoire*. Legislation relating to the latter was discussed in the parliament in Spring 1994, that is *after* the deadline set for the signing of the contracts. Meanwhile, the government used discretionary regional grants as a means of cajoling recalcitrant regions to accept its contractual proposals.

CONCLUSION

Despite the leading role accorded to the DATAR in the territorial planning process and the specificities of contracts for overseas regions, the contractual policy process resembles an aggregation of micro-bargaining, rather than a collective decision-making procedure for regional development. Regional redistribution is only one of the objectives of contractual plans, which contribute to, but do not represent, regional policy. The purpose of contractualization is clearly ambiguous, but the emphasis has steadily moved from regional policy to an institutional technique to regionalize sectoral policies. Other factors have also helped to shape and limit the impact of contractualization. One such issue concerns the organizational coordination of multi-level public policies. Indeed, the integration of regional and European policies is in itself problematic. Admittedly, the EU regional policy procedures are comparable (as they were exported from Paris to Brussels through the Jacques Delors administration), and the prospect of Structural Fund support provides an incentive to contract. However, the policy-making schedules and planning periods vary for regional plans, the national plan (if it exists at all) and each of the Structural Fund Objectives. Moreover, the territorial policy-making process remains highly dependent on political coalitions between levels of government and on electoral cycles. As highlighted above, a change of government may have important implications for the status and direction of regional policy. These difficulties or uncertainties compound the infra-regional tensions outlined above, which have also limited the effective implementation of the *contrats de plan*. What emerges, therefore, is the rather obvious, but no less important fact that any explanation of French territorial policy must take account of the multi-level political configurations which have helped to shape it.

The policy objectives of contractual plans have also followed changes in the cultural context of public policy. Their creation has to be considered in the context of a search for sustained economic development. As the economic crisis has persisted, governments have become more concerned to abandon policy priorities (and financial responsibilities) than to define them. Is it really possible (or sensible) to attempt to implement a redistributive regional policy with an annual growth rate of two per cent when even the more optimistic estimates indicate that a higher rate of economic growth is required? Viewed in this context, *contrats de plan* may be described as a mechanism for managing the redistribution of costs during a period of containment of public expenditure. Thus defined, contractual planning appears as a means of mobilizing the regions behind state policies rather than as a mechanism to provide state support for autonomous regional policies. Though regional politicians bemoaned the financial retreat of the state, they nevertheless continued to sign the *contrats de plan*. They did so for two reasons: the urgency of their needs and the opportunities the contracts provided for regions to extend their policy-making competence. They were thus caught in a revolving door; despite their protests, they could not now withdraw, for instance, from undertakings to finance secondary schools and universities. Moreover, despite these constraints, regions have begun to establish new relationships with organized interests, other local authorities, prefects and central administrations. In retrospect, contractual planning has helped to strengthen the regional institutions. More importantly perhaps, it has also created a new regional polity, that is, a core for a joint policy-making, the main feature of which is inter-organizational relations. More specifically, contractualization has established an evolving network of relationships, within which the position of actors is negotiated, according to political circumstances, through the formulation and implementation of territorial policies including the *contrats de plan*. The state obviously remains the dominant actor within the relationship, but by placing these negotiations at the heart of centre-periphery relations, the 1982 regional reforms have introduced an important shift within the politico-administrative hierarchy.

NOTES

1. Regional prefects are members of the prefectoral corps closely associated with the territorial organization of the French state in departments. The regional prefect is a senior position and is normally held in conjunction with that of prefect of the most populous department within the region.
2. This ratio = State contribution divided by regional contribution.

REFERENCES

Carsalade, Y., 1989, 'La Première Génération de Contrats de Plan Etat-Régions 1984-1988', *Les Contrats de Plan Etat-Régions, Les Cahiers du Centre National de la Fonction Publique Territoriale*, 29 décembre, pp.47-56.

Commissariat Général au Plan, Délégation à l'Aménagement du Territoire et à l'Action Régionale, 1991, *Evaluation des procédures contractuelles en faveur du développement régional*, Projet de Rapport, Document Interne, 15 juillet.

Commissariat Général du Plan, 1985, *Evaluation de la Planification décentralisée* (Paris: La Documentation Française).

Conseil Economique et Social, 1991, *La Planification Régionale* (Rapport présenté par M. Emile Arrighi de Casanova, Séances des 26 et 27 mars), Journal Officiel de la République Française.

Conseil Economique et Social, 1989, *L'articulation des politiques européenne, nationale et régionale d'aménagement du territoire* (Rapport présenté par M. Etienne Simon, Séances des 25 et 26 avril), Journal officiel de la République Française.

De Lanversin, J., A. Lanza and F. Zitouni, 1989, *La Région et l'Aménagement du Territoire dans la Décentralisation* (Paris: Economica).

Lehericy, J., 1989, 'Les Contrats de Plan Etat-Régions de l'Exercice 1989-1993: Présentation Générale', *Les Contrats de Plan Etat-Régions, Les Cahiers du Centre National de la Fonction Publique Territoriale*, nouvelle série,no.29 décembre, pp.76-93.

Madiot, Y., 1989, 'Les Contrats de Plan, une technique juridique', *Les Contrats de Plan Etat-Régions, Les Cahiers du Centre National de la Fonction Publique Territoriale*, nouvelle série,no.29, pp.10-18.

Moreau, J., 1989, 'Les Contrats de Plan Etat-Région, Technique nouvelle d'Aménagement du Territoire?', *Actualité Juridique du Droit Administratif*, 20 Décembre.

Quermonne, J. L., 1963, 'Vers un régionalisme fonctionnel?', *Revue Française de Science Politique*, Vol.13, No.4.

Regional Economic Policies: An Alternative to French Economic Dirigisme?

PATRICK LE GALÈS

There is considerable debate and disagreement over the impact of French regional economic development policies. Are French regions becoming more dynamic and more powerful *en route* to a future Europe of the regions? Or is their influence still marginal? This question applies as much to the economic as to the political domains. On the one hand, Chevallier [*1993*] enthusiastically celebrates the growing importance of the regions and their increased economic role. On the other, Nemery [*1992*] wonders whether regions play any significant economic role at all. Part of the confusion derives from the existence of two different analytical approaches to the study of regions. Economic analyses of French regions stress the growing importance of territory in promoting economic development and then go on to assess the importance of the region within this framework. Opinions vary on this point. Some studies point to the strength of some economic regions and, on this basis, predict a bright future for the development of regional economic policies. This view is opposed by those who believe that regional policies are largely irrelevant to the process of economic development. Other evaluations, based upon an institutional model of regional development emphasise either the increasing power of regions or their lack of powers.

This paper attempts to trace these different arguments. It also examines the economic actions of the regions in the wider context of actions undertaken by public authorities generally – municipalities, departments and the state – to promote local economic development (whatever the level). The argument presented here is that, despite attempts to provide some guidelines for regional economic development, French regional economic policies are, with few exceptions, poorly developed and insignificant. Regional economic policies as they currently exist, do not constitute a viable alternative to former economic strategies based upon French *dirigisme*.

Trigilia [*1991*] seeks to integrate the economic and institutional approaches outlined above. He attempts to show the need for an 'intermediate' level of government to meet the increasing demand for regional regulation in advanced capitalist societies. However, as he goes on to argue, the present institutional framework and regional organization of interests do not necessarily match this need, as highlighted by the case of

Italy. The following discussion applies Trigilia's approach to an analysis of French regions.

TERRITORY AS A FACTOR OF ECONOMIC DEVELOPMENT, REGIONS AT THE HEART OF THE NEW ECONOMIC SYSTEM?

The 're-emergence of regional economies' [*Amin and Robins, 1990*] has been the subject of much debate. One approach has rediscovered space and territory as important variables in explaining economic development [*Pecqueur, 1986*]. Italy and its industrial districts became the focus of much research into local and regional economic development. Several studies of these concluded that local networks and local cultural conditions were important in facilitating the development of non-market exchanges and regulations. These in turn prompted innovation, diffusion of innovation, industrial adaptation and economic development.

Similar conclusions emerged from the other major reference point of the period: the Silicon valley. The science park fever which spread throughout western countries during the 1980s is based on the idea that cross-fertilization between research and firms in the field of high technologies, innovation transfers between various sorts of firms, and an ideological commitment to modern, high tech firms was the best way forward. Again, as far as public policy is concerned, the lesson derived from the mythical valley was to build a science park with a modern communications system [*Storper, 1993*].

These two examples of local economic development have come to constitute the new credo of most regional economists. Although networks of firms are not necessarily localized, that is, the social construction of markets does not need to be related to a particular territory, the Italian case and others demonstrated that this sort of dynamic relationship was more likely to exist in specific, social systems, regions or localities.

Italy and Germany are the principal sources of ideas related to the emergence of forms of 'regional corporatism'. According to this model, the region – rather than the state – becomes responsible for the regulation of economic interests. This is a bold hypothesis, which implies that the region is not merely an institutional construction, but also an economic and social actor. As such, regions thus become the reference point for the definition of corporatist-style relations between economic interests and state organizations. Crouch and Dore [*1990:3*] describe corporatism as:

> An institutionalised pattern which involves an explicit or implicit bargain (or recurring bargaining) between some organ of government and private interest groups (including those promoting 'ideal interests'-causes), one element in the bargain being that the groups

receive certain institutionalised or ad hoc benefits in return for guarantees by the groups' representatives that their members will behave in certain ways considered to be in public interest.

The regions in France thus emerged as the obvious level at which to promote economic development since they were closer to small firms than the state. Indeed, Bernard Ganne [*1994*] has analyzed the role of the French state in relation to small firms over the last 60 years. His stimulating analysis highlights the parallel development of French politico-administrative regulatory systems and macro-economic policy. He identifies four phases of political economy 'governance' in France:

1. The period between the two world wars, when the centralization of the state and its conservatism went hand in hand with vertical political integration and the defence of politically fragmented powers (the famous *notables*) and small firms, sometimes organized as networks.
2. The period of the modernizing state in the 1950s and 1960s, when the national planning system prompted economic restructuring, the modernization and concentration of most economic sectors and the demise of small firms, including small firm networks – during this period the triumphant *dirigiste* state supported only large (often public) firms to build a powerful French industrial base.
3. The period of economic crisis in the 1970s, when the *dirigiste* state had to support major firms and became '*l'Etat-brancardier*' [*Cohen, 1989*]. Small and middle size firms attracted some attention, but insufficient funding. The state developed some early, limited forms of links with local authorities, (partly in response to the demands for support from small firms).
4. The 1980s when small- and middle-size firms were placed at the heart of economic policy in parallel with the decentralization reforms and the mobilization of local authorities.

In the last decade, the problems and failures of some major industrial companies, together with the visible decline in the economic power of the state, paved the way for new initiatives (at both the national and local levels) in support of small firms. It was widely assumed that the end of the French *dirigiste* state would prompt the emergence of an important level of regional economic policy to support networks of firms and to create the right sort of conditions for economic development. The 1982 decentralization reforms lent further weight to this view. Some authors [*Chevallier, 1993*] therefore attributed the glorious forward march of the regions to their increasing economic importance. French regional economic policy thus became the flavour of the month. However, this analysis of the relationship between regional development and economic policy is open to dispute. It was, for instance, clear that the regions had no opportunity, no power and probably very little will to influence international companies or the bigger French firms. By contrast, the *PME* (small- and middle-size firms) were obviously easier to approach. In other words, economic change and new trends in industrial organization (as identified in Italy and the Silicon Valley), plus the intellectual legitimacy given to this model of development by regional economists provided a context within which it was possible to conceive of a *regional* economic policy, albeit one linked to state economic policy. There are therefore at least two dimensions to consider when examining the significance of regional economic policy in different countries: (1) support to firms and (2) regional social and/or economic regulations. In France, in most cases, regions fare badly along both of these dimensions, especially compared with other levels of government, notably the state and municipalities.

REGIONAL ECONOMIC DEVELOPMENT POLICY COMES OF AGE?

In the 1950s, in Alsace and Brittany, regional economic and political elites set up regional lobbies such as the *Association pour le développement et l'industrialisation de la région Alsace* (ADIRA) and the *Comité de Liaison des Intérêts bretons* (CELIB) and demanded the introduction of regionalized economic planning. The French state responded to these pressures with the creation of various instruments and policies. These included the creation of *Sociétés de Développement Régional* (SDR), financial institutions in charge of supporting regional economic development and the introduction of a territorial development policy under the direction of the DATAR set up in 1963.

In the 1960s, *Comités d'Expansion* mushroomed all over France to pave the way for economic decentralization, that is, to prepare sites for firms who were expected to leave Paris. These committees were usually linked to the departments. After 1968, growing regionalist demands, administrative pressures and planning ambitions prompted President Pompidou's governments to introduce further regional reforms and EPRs (*établissements publics régionaux*) were set up. Local and regional politicians built significant alliances with representatives of economic interests which enabled the region to exploit national policies, develop regional plans and offer a degree of regional public support to firms in difficulty.

However, the economic crisis of the mid-1970s boosted demands from EPRs and regionalist groups for the regional authorities to be given more economic powers [*Le Galès, 1989*]. Rising unemployment signalled the end of the all powerful economic state. It gradually lost legitimacy as the only public actor in the field of economic development. Regional political elites resented the fact that citizens expected them to respond to the crisis yet they lacked the means to do so. Their frustration was fuelled on the left, by demands for decentralization of the state and the then popular ideology of *autogestion*, sometimes considered as a possible alternative to the crisis of capitalism. Some regions began to intervene either directly or indirectly in areas of extreme economic crisis despite renewed government warnings that such initiatives were not permitted. The situation was finally acknowledged by the Barre government in the late 1970s which granted limited powers of intervention to EPRs in July 1977 and further extended them in January 1981. Under the strict guidance and control of prefects, the regional authorities were henceforth allowed to give grants (PRCE – *Prime régionale à la création d'emploi*) to regional industries and guarantee loans for small firms.

When the decentralization reforms were passed by Parliament in 1982 and 1983, the role of the region as an economic actor was considered in various ways. Building on the decentralist trends of the 1970s, some argued for strong regions with important economic powers as an alternative to state economic *dirigisme*. Nevertheless, during the first period of the Socialist government, state-led, economic *dirigisme* remained very much at the forefront of the economic agenda [*Cohen, 1989*]. Even so, many considered the newly-established region as the principal partner of the state in the field of economic policy. This view was reflected in the introduction of the *Contrats de Plan Etat-Région* (see chapter by Richard Balme in this volume) which developed what had begun by the *Circonscription d'Action Régionale* and the progressive regionalization of the national economic plan in the 1960s. Thus, economic powers granted to the regions in 1982 gave legal recognition to what had already been happening during the preceding decade.

The creation of regions as full local authorities (*collectivités territoriales*) in 1982, was seen as a major plank of the decentralization reforms. The laws on *interventions économiques des collectivités locales* and, above all, of the regions suggested that the time had finally arrived for regional economic policy. However, even then it was not clear whether the government really supported decentralization, or if it regarded decentralization as a useful means of diffusing responsibility for problems such as unemployment [*Préteceille, 1988*].

'L'INTERVENTION ÉCONOMIQUE DES RÉGIONS': THE GREAT ILLUSION?

'Economic interventions of regions' is a phrase which relates precisely to the legal framework for intervention as defined in the decentralization reforms. The French debate on local authorities' economic policies is often limited to the narrow boundaries defined by the decentralization laws. This legal framework has been analyzed elsewhere [*Douence, 1988 and 1992*]. Douence has convincingly argued that the juridical framework of the regions is redundant to serious analysis of regional economic policies. This point was also emphasized in the case of the municipalities [*Le Galès, 1993*]. Similarly, legal provisions are of no help whatsoever in the case of the departments, which have no specific powers in terms of economic development. Some new powers were given to the regions including training, regional planning and the power to promote economic development. With regard to the latter, the theoretical leadership of the regions was clearly defined; no other local authority was allowed to give direct grants to firms, though there is no formal hierarchy between local authorities. In practice, things did not turn out quite this way.

Despite the legal boost they had received, regions remained remarkably weak in the field of economic development. Formally, they were given the power to give indirect and direct grants to firms, though the latter are subject to tighter legal controls. The regions are allowed to allocate two different types of grant: a PRCE up to a maximum of FF150,000 per firm and a PRE (*prime régionale à l'emploi*) up to a maximum of FF40,000 per employee (for up to 30 employees per firm). They may also provide subsidized accommodation and make long-term loans or financial advances to firms, and give loan guarantees. This does not give regions much scope to design and implement a regional policy. The legal framework is too narrow (especially with regard to the allocation of regional grants) to permit the development of such a policy.

Moreover, notwithstanding the consistent growth of regional budgets over the last decade, regions still have small budgets. Optimists point to the growth in regional budgets over the last decade as evidence of their new importance. It is true that, between 1982 and 1991, the increase in regional budgets was three times greater than that of departmental budgets. The rise was particularly spectacular in the late 1980s; in 1989 the annual increase in regional budgets was 40 per cent. It is commonly assumed that this trend will continue over the next decade and that regions will by implication become major institutional players [*Rangeon, 1993*]. However, an alternative scenario suggests a less bright future for the regions. In 1993, serious budgetary disputes emerged in many regions. In Rhône-Alpes and

Brittany, proposals for tax increases met with widespread opposition. Some right-wing leaders and business interest representatives opposed all tax increases and argued that the steady expansion of regional budgets had to stop. They were supported by some trade-union leaders and Socialist regional councillors (whose opposition to tax increases owed much to the fact that the left controlled only two of the 22 regional councils). In some regions, a powerful chairman such as Charles Millon of Rhône-Alpes, was able to get the budget accepted, albeit by a narrow majority. Elsewhere, however, regional budgetary expansion was strictly contained. Moreover, other local authorities and state representatives generally share the view that regional expenditure and taxes should no longer be permitted to grow at a faster rate than that of other local authorities. The golden age of regional expenditure is thus probably over. Regional budgets are significant, but generally smaller than those of the departments and municipalities.

Regional economic powers are strictly limited. Moreover, they are also defined in such an ambiguous, defensive and uncertain way that regions have been reluctant to use these powers. Instead, many regions have preferred to rely upon their 'general powers' to manage regional affairs in the interest of inhabitants, a trend reinforced by the uncertainties of legal control. Other regions have simply given up. Both solutions reveal the irrelevance of the current legal framework to the realities of regional economic intervention. This framework was modified by the 5 January 1988 law on the *amélioration de la décentralisation*. This, however, did little to reinforce the economic capacity of the region: regional intervention is still required to follow the state's own development priorities and no attempt has been made to enforce cooperation between various level of local authorities. This is made clear by an analysis of regional economic development budgets as shown in Table 5:1.

The figures in Table 5:1, however interesting, should be interpreted with caution. First, the content of the budget line 'economic interventions' varies quite a lot between regions. Moreover, many initiatives are managed by bodies such as regional development agencies, semi-public agencies (*Sociétés d'Economie Mixte*), *associations* or organizations such as Chambers of Commerce and Industry, or financial institutions (*Sociétés de Développement Régional* or *Instituts de Participation*), intended to assist the creation of small firms. Regional expenditure via different agencies tends to lack transparency and often does not appear under the 'economic development' heading of the budget. Legal control over regional budgets is also weak. Despite these limitations, regional budgets do provide us with some useful data.

First, economic development budgets have not increased as much as other types of regional expenditure but underwent a relative decline between 1986

TABLE 5:1
REGIONS' INVESTMENTS FOR ECONOMIC DEVELOPMENT

	Average per inha. 1986/1991 (Francs)	Rate of growth (constant Francs) 1986/1991	Franc/ inhabitant 1991	Total 1986/1991
Limousin	97	+ 10,21%	128	394,719
Mid-Pyrénées	90	+ 6,46%	109	1,230,816
Auvergne	79	+ 8,39%	96	584,692
Bretagne	75	+ 11,94%	89	1,185,00
Poitou-Charentes	67	+ 3,18%	72	601,000
Basse-Normandie	65	+ 7,37%	78	508,210
Bourgogne	63	+ 14,38	91	574,474
Champagne-Ardennes	60	+ 24,30	95	462,223
Franche-Comté	59	+ 24,66	79	367,700
Lorraine	59	+ 12,62	75	763,576
Pays de Loire	52	+ 12,80	63	891,576
Alsace	51	+ 18,14	74	469,161
Languedoc-Roussillon	51	+ 6,09	48	599,374
Picardi	40	+ 21,99	56	411,296
Rhône-Alpes	39	+ 7,25	47	1,176,530
Nord-Pas-de-Calais	35	+ 0,26	37	776,063
Haute-Normandie	33	+ 3,59	36	320,517
Provence-Alpes-Côtes-d'Azur	32	- 1,65	32	758,546
Aquitaine	25	+ 4,28	31	389,271
Centre	12	- 2,99	13	164,200
Ile-de-France	8	+ 26,72	19	511,100
Corse	211	+ 2,91	212	295,667
TOTAL	**42**	**+ 9,40**	**53**	**13,435,711**

Source: DGCL, *Les Echos*, 'L'audit des regions', Isabelle de Gaulmyn, 12 March 1992.

and 1991. Regional economic intervention has also declined in comparison with that of the municipalities and departments. Compared with other regional responsibilities such as building secondary schools, regions have demonstrated little enthusiasm for economic intervention. As Morvan noticed [*Morvan, 1992*], regional expenditure under the heading economic intervention (in the legal sense) formerly represented 10-15 per cent of all local authority expenditure in this category. Nowadays it accounts for only 5-10 per cent.

It is also important to note the economic differences between regions, although this is often difficult because of the absence of comparative data. Nevertheless, figures from Table 5:1 reveal a marked contrast between regions where the level of expenditure is high (Limousin, Midi-Pyrénées, Auvergne, Bretagne and, more recently, Bourgogne and Champagne-Ardennes) and the richest industrial regions. In some cases, ideological factors have served to limit regional economic intervention (Centre, Picardie). However, it is no coincidence that several of the regions which spend little on economic intervention are also the wealthiest regions (Provence-Alpes-Côtes d'Azur, Rhône-Alpes and Haute-Normandie). Regional expenditure on economic development in these regions constitutes between five and ten per cent of total regional expenditure. The wealthiest of all the French regions, Ile-de-France is in a class of its own in this respect: less than one per cent of the regional budget is allocated to economic development.

Regions have gradually abandoned the practice of giving direct grants to firms. These grants initially appeared as the main economic power of regions, but are now seen as inefficient, expensive, and particularly vulnerable to political pressure and clientelism. In reality, the real impact of these grants, good or bad, remains to be seen. In the absence of a clear evaluation process, opinions on the value of direct grants tend to vary in accordance with ideology and the wealth of the region in question. Brittany is a region characterized by a high level of economic intervention, though regional leaders acknowledge they are uncertain of the real impact of such intervention. Nevertheless, they argue that the fragmentation of Brittany's economic base and the large number of small family firms require either some collective organization within the private sector or the support of the public sector including regional councils. The continuous dynamism of small- and middle-size firms in Brittany does not prevent consistent transformation and concentration. Thus, regional grants may have some positive impact here because of the diversity, fragility and rapid change of the regional economic *milieu*. It is therefore argued that the region has no choice but to provide as much support as possible for these firms. Councillors in Socialist-led Limousin also argue that, given the scale of the region's economic problems, they are bound to use all possible means to promote economic development without worrying too much about the precise impact of these measures. In Brittany, some councillors would also argue that they have chosen to have a smaller regional bureaucracy than elsewhere, thereby releasing more available resources to support firms.

By 1992, only six regions used direct grants as defined in the decentralization reforms, compared with 22 regions in 1985. This has led some analysts to conclude that regions have given up their economic functions. In fact, one survey of regional economic policies has confirmed, regions have largely abandoned earlier attempts to exercise ill-defined powers within a narrow legal framework [*Kukawka, 1989*]. Instead, they now concentrate on improving the environment of firms and on more prestigious and symbolic actions, such as supporting the development of new technologies and promoting international cooperation [*Kukawka, 1989*].

INDIRECT METHODS TO SUPPORT ECONOMIC DEVELOPMENT: DO
WIDESPREAD INITIATIVES CONSTITUTE A REGIONAL ECONOMIC POLICY?

French regional elites have not given up all idea of regional economic
development policy. Given the financial, political and legal constraints
imposed upon them by the 1982 decentralization reforms, they have sought
to promote regional development by other means, notably through new
programmes and 'networking'. The diversity of what has been achieved is
quite remarkable. Morvan [*1992*] has identified 149 types of regional action
to support economic development. Chevallier [*1993*] has also argued that
regions have moved away from crude, direct economic development
strategies (grants and loans) to more sophisticated, indirect methods. The
key question, therefore, is how significant are these new means of regional
intervention.

First, although they were accorded few specific powers, regions took
advantage of the 'general powers' which all French local authorities possess.
These powers permit local authorities to develop new initiatives, new
programmes and new domains of intervention, provided that such measures
do not conflict directly with the interests and the powers of the state. Several
regions have assumed a high profile role in promoting new technologies. In
Languedoc-Roussillon for example, the major economic project of the
region is the *Multipole technologique régional*. This seeks to establish links
between high-tech research and industries in eight centres. The official
rationale for this project is threefold: to favour technological transfers from
research centres to small and middle-sized firms; to promote economic
growth in many, small, urban centres within Languedoc-Roussillon; and to
prevent the entrepreneurial mayor of Montpellier from seizing economic
control of the region from the rural *notables*. In 1991, Languedoc-
Roussillon region spent FF6 million on this project out of FF32 million
designated for economic intervention (the total budget of the region was
FF1.7 billion in 1991). An independent study of this particular policy
offered a rather different explanation for regional intervention in this area
[*Ritaine, 1991*]. This argued that new technologies and fierce *pratiques
développementalistes*, that is, economic competition between local
authorities, has stimulated the latter into promoting a new identity for a
region whose economy and elites emerged from the wine business.
G. Frèche, mayor of Montpellier, was the first to promote this policy.
Gradually, both the department and the region responded and followed the
Montpellier development model. According to Ritaine, Languedoc-
Roussillon economic policy is therefore the regional response to the
Montpellier science park strategy, just as the right-wing chairman of the
region, J. Blanc, is also the main political rival to the mayor of Montpellier.
Significantly, however, the new game and strategy was defined by the elites
of the capital city – the region responded to it.

Many regions have focused upon new technologies for symbolic reasons: they appear modern, useful, efficient and are often located in well-designed buildings. Modern technologies are also clean in environmental terms and appeal to the middle-classes. Although it is difficult to evaluate the economic impact of such a strategy, its potential value is rarely disputed in the light of the Silicon Valley myth. Initiatives designed to promote new technologies, firms and research centres usually represent the 'shop window' of regional economic policy. The chairman of the Provence-Alpes-Côtes d'Azur region, J. C. Gaudin, defines his main economic strategy as being to develop science parks, and to strengthen research and science centres. Grants (PRE and PRCE) were abandoned in 1987. The region has since adopted a southern European development strategy based on new technologies (as in the US around Boston) located in the six existing or future science parks of the region. The idea of the *route des hautes technologies* astutely avoids a conflict between the regional capital, Marseilles, which requires some support, and the rest of the region. The cost of the programme is FF1.75 billion over five years, to be paid jointly by the region, the European Union and the state. The region is financing major infrastructure installations such as telecommunications networks and scientific centres. In some cases, the regional council was directly involved in the creation of a science park as in the *Caen/Basse Normandie technopole*. Similarly, in Lorraine, the region played an essential role in the creation of the science park METZ 2000. In this particular case, regional involvement in the project was helped by the fact that the regional chairman was also mayor of Metz and was subsequently appointed to a ministerial post. By contrast, the Ile-de-France regional council provided no assistance for the *Cité d'Orsay* project.

According to Pontier [*1991*], regional research policies generally complement state priorities. Support for research appears to be highest in those regions where such activity has been absent. The economic weight of the region is not a relevant factor. Rhône-Alpes, for example, is willing to support research, whereas Ile-de-France does not feel the need to intervene (as research is already highly concentrated in the Paris region). In Brittany, the regional council has started its own research programme (BRITTA) which is directly related to the needs of regional industries. BRITTA finances research, technology transfers and applied research within firms in the field of biotechnology. This programme received FF35 million from the region in 1991. Poitou-Charentes also funds research contracts with research centres and *grandes écoles*.

Although direct grants are no longer popular, regions still have a variety of schemes to support firms by more indirect means. Many regions, for instance, still provide loan guarantees, or have a fund from which firms may borrow money at favourable rates. These are managed by other organizations such as Chambers of Commerce, public-private partnerships, or even the state field services. Many schemes are in fact jointly financed by the state and the region, including the FRAC (*Fonds régional d'aide au conseil*) which pays the consultancy fees of small firms and funds export schemes. Strictly speaking, these are national schemes co-financed by regions. However, each region tends to give a different name to the same scheme and proudly present it as yet another, new, economic initiative from the region. Promoting exports is now a popular regional strategy which fits well with the willingness of regions to develop an international role. Brittany, for instance, is very active in this field. In 1983, the region created a special body (MIRCEB – *Mission régionale de coordination du commerce extérieur breton*), which currently receives 80 per cent of its resources from the region, that is, FF10 million per year. Alsace also has a fund for firms to employ consultants and its own scheme to boost exports (FREX). Picardie has created an economic development regional agency (ARD) and an agency for exports (AREX).

Regions also play an indirect economic role in other ways. They have become actively involved in international relations. Cooperation between European and French regions has flourished, boosted by EU support and programmes (see also chapter by Mazey in this volume). Well known examples of such cooperation include the SAARLORLUX Euroregion (comprising the regions Saar, Luxembourg and Lorraine), *le quadrige européen*, otherwise known as the four motors of Europe (Rhône-Alpes, Catalonia, Baden-Württemberg and Lombardy), and cooperation between Midi-Pyrénées and Catalonia. More recently, the Atlantic Arc brings together those regions close to the Atlantic, including Brittany, Pays de Loire, Poitou-Charentes and Aquitaine [*Balme and Le Galès, 1993*]. All these networks have resulted in more or less developed economic and cultural cooperation and exchanges between firms. Interregional cooperation of this kind has sharply increased over the last decade; every French region now has links with a region in Europe, Eastern Europe or China. Regions have also opened offices in Brussels, either alone or in association with other regions. Some regions have also opened offices in the US, Japan or Korea in order to attract export orders. Regions are also responsible for preparing the regional plan, which represents the base upon which a negotiation takes place with the state for the decentralized *plan état-région* (see also chapter by Balme in this volume).

Regions have become more interventionist with regard to local development. In Rhône-Alpes and Bourgogne for instance, the region negotiates a local, global plan for small towns or rural areas (often linked to EU programmes), in order to support the development of some areas and to encourage cooperation between small communes. Most regions tend to favour rural areas for political reasons. First, many councillors represent these areas. Second, most regional councils are controlled by right-wing parties, whilst some major cities are controlled by the left. Even when strong mayors and the regional chairperson have similar political allegiances, relations between the municipality and the region may be difficult (as in Limousin or Rhône-Alpes). Nord-Pas-de-Calais is exceptional in this respect, because it is an urban region with a long-standing tradition of regional intervention in favour of urban regeneration. Overall, despite the increasing role played by some regions in the field of local development, the department is the leading actor in the fields of policy.

Training is an essential issue for regions. Some Italian and German authors argued that training was an obvious task for regions [*Trigilia, 1991*]. They argued that regions are the right sort of institution to regulate various interests involved in training. The 1982 decentralization reforms accorded the region important powers in the field of training. However, evaluation of regional training policy is not an easy task. The difficulty derives from the lack of comparative empirical data and the increasing differences between regions in this sector. Superficially, it appears that regions spend considerable sums of money on training and it is easy to argue that they have taken the lead in training. Through training, regions have also established a working relationship with firms, trade-unions and numerous public and private agencies. Some would even argue that regional training policies have been successful in overcoming the long-standing problem of fragmentation of training programmes in France. Several regions were keen to emphasize this point during the 1992 regional elections, and some of the more innovative regions in this field (for example, Rhône-Alpes, Poitou-Charentes) even suggested a new round of decentralization to enhance further the leadership of regions in this field. Some regions have gone so far as to create a department of training and to employ professional advisers.

However, closer inspection of regional training programmes reveals a rather different picture. Michel's [*1994*] study of Brittany's training policy highlighted the money spent by the region, the symbolic lead taken by regional councillors and identified the emergence of a new credo of regional training. It also confirmed that, contrary to appearances, training policy has remained mainly controlled by the state and professionals and that the region plays only a minor role. First, regional councillors lack detailed knowledge and understanding of training programmes. With one or two exceptions, councillors are not in control of programme design and implementation. The training policy community and its professionals have thus maintained control over the content of programmes. Second, and most importantly, despite the powers given to regions, the state has remained by far the most important player and funds more programmes than the regions. In fact, the new national priorities for training were prepared for the *contrat de plan* by the *commissariat au plan* in 1984 and 1985. Most innovative regional training policy amounts to paying for nationally-designed schemes, and running and building new training centres (politically symbolic). A comparison of training programmes in Brittany with other regional and national schemes revealed an almost total lack of originality – the lack of any regional policy in fact. Third, most programmes are organized in cooperation with various actors and interests and thus offer regions, in theory at least, an opportunity to play a regulatory role. Despite claims by the Brittany regional council that it has a good reputation for regional collective action, the study shows that entrepreneurs were not involved in regional training policy, which remained dominated by professionals. The region also played only a marginal role. The only occasion where the region played a decisive role occurred when it acted as a referee when conflicts arose. Rangeon reached similar conclusions in his analysis of Picardy's training policy [*Rangeon, 1993*]. These cases are probably not exceptional. However, some regions, mainly those controlled by the right-wing UDF, seem to have taken a more active role. Ile-de-France also claims to play a major role in this sector. More positively, Michel [*1994*] concluded that the learning period was over for regional councillors and nothing prevented the region from taking a more active role in this area in the future.

A five year *loi d'orientation sur l'emploi* (*loi* Giraud) was voted by Parliament at the end of 1993. Among other things, it seeks to introduce some regional regulation of training. Bearing in mind the uncertain achievements of earlier attempts to decentralize training, the law stresses that regional training programmes are the way forward. New, decisive powers and budgets have thus been given to regions in an attempt to change the balance of powers between the state and regions in favour of the latter. Regions are also encouraged to seek EU funding for training programmes. This new development raises a number of important questions regarding the future development of training policy. How will the coherence of national and regional programmes be achieved? Is such coherence essential? Will regions try to associate and work with all the actors involved? Will regional policies be properly evaluated (a crucial omission hitherto)? Will regions play the new game and begin to regulate those interests involved in regional training programmes? Answers to these questions will vary from one region to another.

Two conflicting interpretations of the economic importance of regions are possible from the above account. On the one hand, one may argue that regional economic intervention has increased and is bound to continue to increase in the future. Yet, it is also possible to argue that regional economic intervention, though variable, remains largely symbolic and devoid of substance. This article tends to support the second interpretation. Often, analyses of regional policies concentrate solely on regions. Comparing what regions were doing ten years ago with what they do now inevitably leads authors to conclude that regions are becoming important economic actors. The following section presents a different story: the whole world of government has been transformed in the last 15 years. Municipalities, departments and even the state have acquired new roles and responsibilities. Compared with the economic activities of other local authorities and public organizations, regional economic policy appears even more symbolic and insignificant.

THE ECONOMIC ROLE OF MUNICIPALITIES, DEPARTMENTS AND
STATE AGENCIES

As indicated above, regions have taken advantage of the unwritten rule of French local government, namely that each level of local government may intervene in any domain it wishes, irrespective of specific powers accorded to it. However, the same argument applies to departments and municipalities. Departments are, for instance, not supposed to be involved in economic development. However, they are increasingly active in that field. Also, they are closer to the small communes upon whom they tend to impose their priorities within *contrats de plan*. To date, regions have failed to establish any economic or political leadership over departments. Moreover, examination of departmental budgets and actions suggests that departments are at least as active as regions with regard to economic development policies.

A similar, but stronger argument could be made about municipalities (either the principal municipality or the intermunicipal body in charge of the economic policy of the urban area). Having pioneered several economic initiatives in the 1970s, large French cities promoted large-scale economic development policies in the 1980s [*Le Galès, 1993 and 1994*]. It so happens that trends in economic development in France during the 1980s also show a concentration of economic activity in or around cities at the expense of the rest of the region [*Savy and Veltz, 1993*]. Thus, the regional contribution to economic development, though increasing, remains small and relatively insignificant in comparison with other local authorities.

The role played by regions in regulating and organizing socio-economic interests at the regional level also needs to be evaluated in a wider context. Despite the paucity of data on this subject, the role played by departments and municipalities in this respect raises further doubts about the importance of regions. Many business organizations are organized at the departmental and/or local level, but not at the regional level. The growth of private-public partnerships and strategic planning at the local level is a key development of the last ten years. Local actors involved in these processes tend not to care too much for the region.

The development of regional economic policy has often been attributed to the inability of the centralized state to respond to the needs of small firms. However, administrative reform has strengthened the capacity of the state in this respect. The Ministry of Industry underwent a large-scale transformation during the 1980s. As with training policy, some industrial development schemes were designed and proposed by the ministry and then financed (partly by the region) through *contrats de plan*. As local, departmental and regional councillors become increasingly concerned with economic problems, companies often prefer to deal with state officials with no local political interests to defend. Other organizations, such as the ANVAR (*Agence nationale pour la Valorisation de la Recherche*), despite some difficulties, are also active in supporting innovation and innovation transfers for small firms. It is widely agreed that the generous financial contribution given by ANVAR to firms for innovation projects has not always been as effective or controlled as it might have been. Nevertheless, it has indirectly supported many small or middle-size family firms.

Recent schemes such as FRADE (*Formation et Recherche Appliquée au Développement Economique*), created by the DATAR, aim at developing links and partnerships between technical colleges and firms. The region is often a partner in these schemes and some money may be devoted to FRADE in *contrats de plan*. However, the initiative comes from the centre and other local authorities play an important role in the implementation process. State services, from the DATAR to the ANVAR, are also responsible for the management of European programmes supporting firms such as STRIDE. Partnerships between regions and state services are often presented as evidence of the growing importance of the region in promoting economic development. They should, however, be seen as a mechanism for the state to obtain additional funding for its programmes.

The provision of finance for firms is yet another area where the region remains relatively weak. French small- and medium-sized enterprises (PME-PMI), many of which are family-owned, traditionally suffer from a lack of capital. Such firms often lack the solid financial base necessary to survive prolonged periods of economic recession. It has also been argued that the banking system has proved only moderately responsive to the needs of these firms. Since the late 1950s, the *Sociétés de Développement régional* (SDR), created by the state, have played a key role in supporting PME-PMI in French regions. The SDR had become increasingly close to the regions. However, in the last five years, they have faced serious economic difficulties. Particularly important was the loss of their privileged position in the money-lending market. Of the 20 SDR, several have experienced financial difficulties over the last five years and four have narrowly avoided bankruptcy. There is now a serious risk that the SDR network will lose its regional character and become integrated within a national financial organization. Regions would then lose a crucial ally, a financial organization which was also sensitive to their concerns and which supported PME-PMI on a long-term basis. Although regional chairpersons have shown some concern at this prospect, their attempts to support the SDR have so far proved ineffective. This is particularly worrying since even when regions themselves have had the opportunity to support firms by indirect means, they have not been keen to do so.

CONCLUSION

Economic policy defined as actions designed to support economic development in a wide sense, has become a priority for all levels of government, including regions. It appears that regional economic policies though becoming more important, nevertheless remain relatively insignificant, especially in comparison with other local authority actions. This paper has sought to demonstrate that contrary to appearances, regions have not yet become important economic actors. In short, regional economic policies are not a substitute for state intervention. This view nevertheless requires some qualification. The 1982 decentralization reforms did mark an important stage in the development of regional policy in several respects. In particular, the political legitimacy of the region was increased, regions were granted specific powers to intervene in the economy and acquired a potentially important role in the planning process. Moreover, the regions are as yet relatively young (and by implication immature) institutions. As such they have a great capacity for adaptation and innovation (as illustrated by the recent introduction of more effective planning procedures). There are also, of course, significant variations between regions with regard to economic policy. Some wealthy regions, such as Rhône-Alpes, have already become known for their interventionist approach to economic development. Meanwhile, the economic crisis of the past two years has convinced several regions of the need to become more active. Looking to the future, the new *Loi d'Orientation* on training is likely to provide new opportunities for regional mobilization and organization of interests in this domain. European integration (notably EU structural funds and the new EU regional committee) is also likely to give a further boost to regional policy and interregional cooperation. Finally, opinion polls conducted by the *Observatoire interrégional du Politique* suggest that 80 per cent of the population would like regions to be given more powers over training programmes and industrial assistance.

The point remains, however, that regions have not taken an active economic role to date. One may even question the possibility of such a development. Networks of firms are growing, but not necessarily on a territorial basis. It remains to be seen whether such networks can be organized on a territorial, rather than sectoral or professional basis. The completion of the Single European Market will also lead to more economic competition and greater inequalities between regions (see Mazey in this issue). Not all regions will have the necessary resources to play a serious economic role. The development of regional economies remains to be seen as does the development of truly regional economic policies. As far as cooperation with Europe is concerned, any partnership involving local authorities (at several levels) and the state will always lead, in France, to the state being the referee.

It is perhaps appropriate to end by turning once again to the arguments put forward by Trigilia above on the need for an intermediate level of government (or governance) in Western capitalist countries. Trigilia convincingly argues his case and suggests this should be the region, though this is, in fact, not the case in Italy. In France also, the region does not play this role, though the regional paradox outlined at the beginning of this paper, may one day be resolved. However, why should this role be reserved for the region? It could also be the metropolitan area which plays this intermediate role in France. Much more research is needed on this subject. However, there are several arguments which could be put forward in favour of cities as key, local social and economic actors in the new Europe. The now fashionable problem of territorial regulation is central to this debate. The paradox of the regions may prove easier to solve at the metropolitan level. The link between cities and regions thus deserves more attention.

REFERENCES

L'actualité Juridique Droit Administratif, 1992, Special issue, 'Décentralisation : Bilan et Perspectives', April.

Administration, 1992, Special issue, 'L'Etat et les entreprises', 156.

Amin, A. and K. Robins, 1990, 'The re-emergence of regional economies? The mythical geography of flexible accumulation', *Environment and Planning D*, 8, pp.7-74.

Balme, R. and P. Le Galès, 1993, *Stars and black holes, French local authorities and Europe*, Unpublished paper for the network EUROLOG.

Brocard, M. and Y. Rocher, 1990, 'Les régions ont-elles une politique scientifique?', *La Recherche*, n.218, février 1990.

Benko, G. and A. Lipietz (eds), 1992, *Les régions qui gagnent* (Paris: PUF).

Bourjol, M., 1969, *Les institutions régionales de 1789 jusqu'à nos jours* (Paris: Berger-Levrault).

Bouvard, L. and P. Calame, 1988, *Le dialogue des entreprises et du territoire* (Paris: Rapport pour le Ministère de l'Equipement).

Bucaille, A. and B. Costa de Beauregard, 1987, *PMI enjeux régionaux et internationaux* (Paris: Economica).

Chevallier, J., 1993, 'Les compétences régionales', in CURAPP, *Les Politiques régionales* (Paris: PUF).

Cohen, E., 1989, *L'Etat brancardier* (Paris: Calman-Lévy).

Crouch, C. and R. Dore, 1990, 'Whatever happened to corporatism', in C. Crouch and R. Dore (eds), *Corporatism and accountability; organised interests in Britsh public life* (Oxford: Clarendon Press).

CURAPP, 1993, *Les Politiques régionales* (Paris: PUF).

Decoster, E., 1991, 'Les Phénomènes de technopolisation en Ile de France du Sud : les collaborations Recherches-Industries', *Cahiers du GDR 874 CNRS*, 8, pp.5-45.

Dematteis, G., 1993, 'Regioni geografiche, articolazione territoriale degli interessi et regioni istituzionali', *Stato e Mercato*, 27, pp.115-37.

Doeriner, P., D. Terkla and G. Topakian, 1987, *Invisible factors of economic development* (Oxford: Oxford University Press).

Dony-Bartholme, M., 1991, 'Les aides publiques aux entreprises face au droit européen de la concurrence', *Politique et Management Public*, vol.9, no.4, pp.2-22.

Douence, J. C., 1988, *L'action économique locale, décentralisation ou recentralisation* (Paris: Economica).

Douence, J. C., 1991, 'L'action économique locale', *Actualité Juridique et Droit Administratif*, April, pp.68-76.

Drevet, J. F., 1988, *Les régions françaises entre l'Europe et le déclin* (Paris: Souffles).

Dupuy, C. and J. P. Gilly, 1987,'Toulouse et les dynamismes intra-régionaux de Midi-Pyrénées', *Revue géographique des Pyrénées et du Sud-Ouest*, vol.62, no.3, pp.265-84.

Ganne, B., 1994, 'Derrière les PME, l'Etat', in Bagnasco A. and C. Sabel. (eds), (forthcoming), *Small firms in Europe* (London: Frances Pinter).

Giblin, B., 1991, 'Les territoires de la nation: l'heure de la décentralisation et de l'Europe', *Hérodote*, vol. 62, pp.23-43.

Gerbaux, F. and P. Muller, 1992, 'Les interventions économiques des collectivités locales', *Pouvoirs*, 60, pp.99-114.

Gold, D., 1987, 'L'intervention économique de la région Aquitaine: l'exemple des primes à la création d'entreprises et d'emplois', *Revue Economique du Sud-Ouest*, 2, pp.57-80.

Gollain, V. and D. Lecomte, 1991, 'La position concurrentielle de l'Ile-de-France en Europe', *Cahiers de l'IAURIF*, 100, pp.9-23.

Greffe, X., 1984, *Territoires en France, les enjeux économiques de la décentralisation* (Paris: Economica).

Greffe, X., 1988, *Décentraliser pour l'emploi* (Paris: Economica).

Hatzfeld, H., 1991, 'La décentralisation du système éducatif: les régions de l'épreuve, *Politique et Management Public*, 9, 4, pp.24-48.

Kahn, R., 1993, 'Facteurs de localisation, compétitivité et collectivités territoriales', *Revue d'Economie Régionale et Urbaine*, 2, pp.309-26.

Kukawka, P., 1989, 'Les interventions économiques des régions', in S. Wachter (ed.), *Politiques publiques et territoires* (Paris: L'Harmattan).

Lachman, J., 1993, 'Nouvelles stratégies territoriales', *Inter-régions*, 158, pp.22-25.

Laurencin, J. P. and N. Rousier, 1990, 'Une approche territoriale de l'économie régionale dans la perspective de 1993, le cas de la région Rhône-Alpes', *Revue d'économie régionale et urbaine*, 1, pp.83-104.

Leborgne, D. and A. Lipietz, 1988, 'L'après fordisme et son espace', *Les temps modernes*, 501.

Le Cacheux, J. and L. Tourjansky, 1992, 'Dix ans de décentralisation française: éléments de bilan', *Observations et diagnostics économiques Revue de l'OFCE*, 41.

Le Galès, P., 1989, 'Les politiques de développement local', in S. Wachter (ed.), *Politiques publiques et territoires* (Paris: L'Harmattan).

Le Galès, P., 1992, 'New directions in decentralisation and urban policy in France: the search for a post decentralisation state', *Environment and Planning C Government and Policy*, 10, pp.19-36.

Le Galès, P., 1993, *Politique urbaine et développement local, une comparaison franco-britannique* (Paris: L'Harmattan).

Le Galès, P., 1994, 'Questions sur les villes entrepreneurs', in S. Biarez et J. Y. Nevers (eds), *Les politiques urbaines* (Grenoble: Cahiers du CERAT).

Maillard, D., 1993, 'Quelle politique industrielle en 1992?', *Regards sur l'Actualité*, mai, pp.27-39.

Mény, Y., 1974, *Centralisation et décentralisation dans le débat politique français (1945-1969)* (Paris: LGDJ).

Michel, H., 1994, 'Décideurs ou régulateurs? Le cas des élus régionaux chargés de la formation professionnelle en Bretagne', in J. Fontaine et C. Le Bart (eds), *Le métier politique*, (Paris: L'Harmattan).

Morvan, Y., 1990, 'Europe et régions: l'age de l'indifférence, l'âge des compensations, l'âge des coopérations, vers l'âge de raison', *Cahiers Economiques de la Bretagne*, 2, pp.1-10.

Morvan, Y., 1991, 'Aménagement du Territoire et Développement économique: petite histoire d'une rencontre inachevée', *Cahiers Economiques de la Bretagne*, 4, pp.1-8.

Morvan, Y., 1992, 'Six ans d'interventions économiques des régions: un essai de bilan', *Cahiers Economiques de la Bretagne*, 2, pp.1-9.

Nemery, J. C., 1992, 'Régions, départements, communes, la nouvelle donne', *Cahiers Français*, 256.

Nemery, J. C. and S. Wachter (eds), 1993, *Entre l'Europe et la décentralisation* (Paris: Editions de l'Aube/DATAR).

Oberti, M., 1992, *Classes sociales et territoires en Italie*, Unpublished Doctoral thesis, University of Paris X, Nanterre.

Observatoire Interrégional du Politique, 1993, *Les français et leur région. Le fait régional et l'opinion publique* (Paris: La documentation française/DATAR).

Pecqueur, B., 1986, 'Crise économique, crise du discours sur l'espace', *Annales de la Recherche Urbaine*, 29, pp.13-21.

Pecqueur, B., 1991, *Le développement local* (Paris: Syros).

Piore, M. J. and C.F. Sabel, 1984, *The second industrial divide* (New York: Basic Books).

Pontier, J. M., 1991, 'Les régions et la recherche', *La revue administrative*, 262, pp.308-14.

Préteceille, E., 1988, 'Decentralisation in France: new citizenship or restructuring hegemony', *European Journal of Political Research*, 16, pp.403-24.

Rangeon, F., 1993, 'Les politiques régionales, le cas de la Picardie', in CURAPP, *Les Politiques Régionales* (Paris : PUF).

Ritaine, E., 1991, *Changement social et pratiques développementalistes en Languedoc-Roussillon* (Bordeaux: CERVL et Ministère de la Recherche et de la Technologie).

Ross Mackay, R., 1993, 'A Europe of Regions: a role for non-market forces', *Regional Studies*, 27,5, pp.419-31.

Savy, M. and P. Veltz, 1993, *Les nouveaux espaces des entreprises* (Paris: Datar/Editions de l'Aube).

Steib, J., 1987, *Les interventions économiques des collectivités locales*, Rapport du Comité Economique et Social, 3 juin (Paris: La Documentation française).

Storper, M. and A .J. Scott, 1992, *Pathways to industrialisation and regional development* (London: Routledge).

Storper, M., 1993, 'Regional "Worlds" of Production: Learning and Innovation in the Technology Districts of France, Italy and the USA', *Regional Studies*, 27,5, pp.433-55.

Tequeneau, P., 1991, 'Les territoires après la décentralisation: le dessous des cartes', *Hérodote*, 62, pp.44-63.

Triglia, C., 1985, 'La regolazione localistica, economia et politica nelle aree di piccole imprese', *Stato et Mercato*, 14.

Trigilia, C., 1991, 'The paradox of the region: economic regulation and the representation of interests', *Economy and Society*, 20, 3, pp.306-27.

Environmental Policy and the Regions in France

MARYVONNE BODIGUEL and HENRY BULLER

INTRODUCTION

The precipitous regionalization of France in the last 20 years, a '*révolution tranquille*' in the words of historian Jean-Pierre Rioux, has prompted considerable debate within the broader context of political decentralization [*Pouvoirs, 1992*]. Debate centres upon two issues: the extent to which there exists a policy-making justification for a regional tier of local government; and the impact of this additional structure on the other levels of territorial and central administration and government. In the field of environmental policy-making, this debate has added pertinence as the environment is still a relatively new area of political and administrative intervention, both at the central and local levels. Given the general absence of antecedent policy-making and policy-implementing structures specific to the environment, the creation of the regional tier has coincided with the emergence of French environmental policy. The regions therefore occupy a potentially important place both as territorial entities which appear, at first sight, to be intrinsically well adapted to addressing environmental concerns not specific to a particular locality, and as administrative and governmental structures lying between the local level and the central state, or even of the 'super-state' in the form of the European Union. Nevertheless, the French regions are paradoxically endowed with very few specific powers in the environmental policy domain. This state of affairs reflects, we argue here, the equivocal position of the French regions in general as part legitimate territories, part supernumerary policy structures, and part necessary regrouping in an increasingly complex political and administrative landscape.

Territorially, the French regions represent two very distinct sets of political institution, the twin pillars of French administrative and political structure. On the one hand, the region is home to the regional level of local government, composed of the *Conseil régional* and its services. On the other, the region also plays host to certain antennae of the 'deconcentrated' central state. These latter agencies and other bodies, which operate as the regional level representatives of central ministries, are under the immediate responsibility of the regional prefect. Their task is essentially one of ensuring regulatory conformity in local policy and decision-making and they are entirely distinct, in both role and stature, from the local government institutions of the regional council. Indeed, it is strictly speaking a misnomer to refer to them as 'regional' as they remain extensions of the state. Nevertheless, both the regions (the councils and their services) and the regional state services may be regarded as actors in the local environmental policy-making arena operating at the regional level. It would be wrong to treat the latter simply as the unequivocal voice of the relevant national ministry in any analysis of local policy-making, as we demonstrate below.

Our intention in this paper is to explore some of the issues raised by the growing involvement of these two pillars in environmental policy-making at the regional level over the last ten years. Two fundamental questions emerge. First, how does the growth of regional responsibilities in the environmental domain reflect the development of French environmental policy as a whole? In response to this question, we propose to examine the emergence of a regional input into French environmental policy-making by assessing, first, the growth of the specific environmental competencies and responsibilities of the 22 French regional authorities and, second, the role of the regional bureaux of the Ministry of the Environment. A second question concerns the impact of the creation of a regional governmental and administrative tier upon the pre-existing structures of local and central government. Here, we consider, through the example of environmental policy, the effects of regionalization and indeed of the twin processes of political decentralization and state deconcentration. Have these processes, as was intended, brought political decisions in the environmental domain closer to the public?

THE GROWTH OF REGIONAL ENVIRONMENTAL RESPONSIBILITIES

The Environment and Economic Planning

The French regions emerged, in the mid-1950s, as administrative units born of the post-war period of French growth and superimposed upon a cultural and territorial structure that, in certain cases, goes back many centuries. That process of superimposition was, and to a large extent remains, very uneven. Few of the French administrative regions can be said to correspond closely to genuine ethnic identities. Those of Brittany, Alsace and Corsica come perhaps closest to their historical, cultural and ethnic predecessors, though Languedoc-Roussillon, Auvergne and others contain, at least in part, a relatively coherent ethnic heartland. Elsewhere, 'regions' such as Centre, Champagne-Ardennes and Poitou-Charentes have been almost wholly invented.

The formal definition of the regions was made during a critical period of French economic modernization, which has to a large degree characterized their subsequent evolution and crucially influenced their role with respect to environmental policy-making. As defined in the initial legislation of 1955 and later legislation in 1958, 1960, 1964 up until 1972, the regions, or *circonscriptions d'action régionale* as they were then known, were conceived as a necessary regional element to state-led economic and infrastructural planning. In consequence, they had few if any independent policy-making powers, acting essentially as regional forums for identifying economic development and growth priorities.

It is in the light of these very focused regional functions and of the very limited policy-making autonomy of regional administration, that we must assess the development of a regional environmental policy role. Until very recently, the manner in which the regional authorities have addressed environmental policy-making has been strongly influenced both by their essentially economic planning orientation and by the long absence of any real political power at the local level.

As we have argued elsewhere [*Bodiguel, 1991; Buller, 1992*], early French concern for a broad range of environmental issues emerged as an implicit component of the economic and infrastructural planning policies of the 1960s. These policies were originally designed to reduce regional inequalities and maintain an economically viable rural France. They also sought, through the promotion of economic development, to protect the rural environment from degradation as a result of depopulation, to preserve the natural resource base through agricultural practices and to improve the rural amenities of local inhabitants through investment. Consequently, broad land-use planning, or *aménagement du territoire*, must be seen as one of the central thrusts of early French environmental protection policy. Here, the fledgling regions played the key administrative role, one for which they were ultimately conceived. The national administrative agency, *Délégation à l'Aménagement du Territoire et à l'Action Régionale* (DATAR) had, from its creation in 1963 onwards, an essentially regional focus and hence operated in close cooperation with the regional administrations and the regional economic development commissions (CODER) who, through consultation, had a significant voice in the elaboration of the national Plans and in regional planning, and thereby in broad environmental policy-making.

The environmental component of regional planning was always implicit rather than explicit and it is often difficult to tease out from broad planning and development objectives, specific regional environmental responsibilities. However, in one area in particular, regional authorities were able, relatively early on, to benefit from an important policy-making role, one that enabled them to become at last genuine 'tools of decentralized planning'.

The *Parcs naturels régionaux* (PNR) were created in 1967 following considerable lobbying from the DATAR, through its *Commission interministérielle des parcs naturels régionaux*, for a coherent planning tool permitting the reconciliation of environmental and developmental objectives in rural areas. Although the central state still retains the final decision over the designation of individual parks, the 1970s saw the gradual regionalization of PNR policy culminating in the decree of October 1975 which handed both the initiative for the creation of PNRs to the region, subsequent to consultation with the other relevant tiers of local government and with the DATAR, and the overall responsibility for park management. To date, 24 PNRs exist, covering 6.5 per cent of metropolitan France.

This initial phase of regional environmental responsibility was thus characterized by the continuing domination of the central state as ultimate policy- and decision-maker, with the regions performing an essentially proselytizing role. In bringing this regional perspective to national economic and infrastructural planning, the regions did nevertheless import a significant environmental element to national planning prerogatives. The maintenance of an economically and socially sustainable rural France and the protection and amelioration of the amenity of rural residents were, in the France of the 1960s and 1970s, the central environmental concerns. The creation of the PNRs and the emergence of the regional authorities as their principal administrators was the culmination of this, particularly French, approach to environmental policy-making.

Decentralization and Regional Environmental Policy

The decentralization measures of 1982 formally changed the status of the regions from being planning arms of the central state (*établissements publics*) to being a legally defined level of local government (*collectivité territoriale*). The reforms of 1982 gave the regions greater policy-making autonomy arguably in only very limited areas but including the management of waterways, ports and coastlines. Significantly, this area of responsibility has proved to be an important entry point for certain regional agencies, such as those of Languedoc-Roussillon, into environmental policy-making and management.

The emergence of specific environmental responsibilities at the regional level developed relatively late. Indeed, the emergence of a specific environmental responsibility within French government as a whole is a recent phenomenon [*Morand-Deviller, 1987*]. Following decentralization, the regions have a number of general powers of intervention in environmental matters though these are, on the whole, the result less of any specific decentralization of central authority than of the potentialities of their position within the territorial hierarchy [*Prieur, 1988*]. In addition to their long-standing role in initiating, coordinating, financing and managing the *Parcs naturels régionaux* discussed above, we can identify four broad new areas of possibility for post-decentralization regional action in the environmental domain.

First, the regions dispose of a significant initiation and consultation role. Although it may have limited environmental expertise, the region may nonetheless be in a position to offer a specific regional (that is, trans-departmental) perspective to environmental matters [*Romi, 1990*]. Regional intervention of this kind can enable issues otherwise dealt with only in a fragmentary fashion at the departmental level to enter the broader political agenda. One example is provided by the rural planning and environmental problems of central Brittany which have incited a *de facto* regional policy response largely because of the absence of any coherent policy at the sub-regional level.

Second, the incorporation of environmental goals in the state-region partnership economic development plans (*Contrats de Plan Etat-Région*) places the regions in a key position with regard to the financing of environmental programmes. A large number of regions have sought state financial aid for specific environmental actions in this way, notably in the water management and coastline protection sectors [*Conseil régional de Basse-Normandie, 1991*]. Whereas the environment did not emerge as a major theme in the first round of *Contrats de Plan Etat-Région*, the 1990s have seen a growing number of submitted environmental programmes. Without doubt, these have provided the regions with a new and now considerable importance [*Capul, 1985*], though this importance continues to remain essentially consultative and financial. Regulatory powers remain, as they always have been, the prerogative of the state and the regional and departmental prefects. Policy-making powers are now largely held by the individual departments.

Third, and in large part as a consequence of their economic planning functions, French regions have emerged in recent years as major financial partners in local actions and programmes, be they linked to economic development or environmental protection. To some extent, this represents the continuation of a policy of financial partnership developed with the *Contrats de pays* of the 1970s. However, the recent creation of a widening series of voluntary environmental planning documents (for example, the *plans municipaux d'environnement*, the *plans départementaux d'environnement*, the *schémas d'aménagement et de gestion des eaux*), reform of intermunicipal structures in 1992, and the growing involvement of regions in promoting local environmental sensibilities have undoubtedly raised the regions' profile in both the environmental and land-use planning fields [*Logié, 1992*]. The region of Picardie for example, under its '*projet territoire*', is currently seeking to encourage, through the creation of a regional local development fund, local environmental initiatives at an intercommunal level.

Fourth, and like the above, crucial to their expanding political functions, the regions have become *de facto* intermediaries between local government and the European Union. This development has occurred as a result of political decentralization and as a consequence of the European Union's own need for access to a suitably sized representative level of European localities. The regions are benefiting from this privileged position as they administer European structural fund monies and, to a certain degree, have an influence over the submission of programmes and projects by individual departments to Brussels. This recent responsibility has given the regions a critical role in both helping to define and, in effect, adapting, local environmental policy to European criteria [*Blumann, 1989*].

The Region and the State

Accompanying the aforementioned process of political decentralization, and as a crucial adjunct to it, the legislation of 1982 saw the local services of a number of state ministries deconcentrated to the regions and departments and placed under the authority of the respective prefects. To balance the greater freedom enjoyed by local governments, the state has strengthened its position at the regional and departmental levels by permitting a certain number of regulatory decisions to be taken locally rather than in Paris. To a certain extent therefore, the decentralization reforms of the 1980s have brought the state closer to the citizen, while the citizen has become more independent of the state through the process of political decentralization.

The regional tier is host to the local bureaux of the Ministry of the Environment. Unlike other ministries, such as, most notably, those of Planning and Infrastructure (*Equipement*) and Agriculture, the Ministry of the Environment has no distinct bureaux at the departmental level. Thus, the *Directions régionales de l'environnement* (DIREN), created in 1991 following the combining of the former *Délégués régionaux à l'Architecture et à l'Environnement* (DRAE) and the *Services régionaux de l'aménagement de l'eau* (SRAE – formerly under the tutelage of the Ministry of Agriculture), have become the sole territorial element in governmental environmental policy-making and regulation. The DIREN reveal, in their own weaknesses, many of the inadequacies of their parent ministry. Baptized, soon after its birth, as the 'ministry of the impossible' [*Poujade, 1975*], the Ministry of the Environment has, throughout its 22-year history, struggled to find a suitable and effective position within the administrative and ministerial structure of France. The multiplication of environmental problems of an international scale and the growth within France of environmental issues of increasingly popular concern, such as that of waste disposal, water quality and river management, have allowed the Ministry of the Environment to achieve a certain prominence. However, its exact functions have remained largely ill-defined and its form has been in a virtually perpetual state of reorganization.

At the regional level, the DIREN are under the authority of the regional or the departmental prefect according to the geographical scale of the issues addressed. Following decentralization, environmental competencies were allocated in blocks to the various levels of local government (municipalities, departments and regions). The department is responsible for protected natural area policy, though the DIREN may also intervene in their capacity as the ministry's regional directorate. The DIREN organize, coordinate and, where necessary, undertake the collection, utilization and diffusion of data and knowledge relative to the environment. They participate in the choice and implementation of appropriate methods for the management, planning and protection of the natural milieu and its resources while seeking to adapt these methods to the regional context (art. 5, decree of 4 November 1991). In addition to this comprehensive mission, the DIREN are also charged with a variety of tasks which collectively endow them with a broad orchestrating function. They oversee local economic planning documents, they are charged with applying legislation relating to water protection, historic site management, nature protection, architectural and civic heritage, environmental impact studies, and are responsible for increasing public environmental awareness. Finally, they too contribute to the preparation and implementation of the State-Region Plans where these relate to environmental issues.

The regional environment director, as head of the DIREN, should, according to the relevant legal texts, participate as fully as possible in the actions of the regional government though, as yet, it is far too early to judge how this provision works in practice. The environment is a crucial issue at the regional level as it necessarily enters other policy areas such as those of economic strategy, planning and water. The creation of the DIREN and the associated transfer of environmental competencies to the regional level therefore represents, in theory at least, a significant entry point into these other policy areas. Any environmental administration thus has a potentially major role to play within regional policy formulation.

The DIREN might become important contributors to environmental policy-making within the territorial ensemble that makes up the French regions, but can they become genuinely accepted in their transversal role of monitoring, regulating, providing advice and information and undertaking or commissioning research? All these tasks have to be undertaken subject to the attributions of other external services of the state and competent state agencies. Such attributions include those of the services of the Ministries of Agriculture, Equipment, Transport and Culture operating, according to the different issues, at both the regional and the departmental levels. The regional environment director is therefore required to perform the role of general environmental policy coordinator. As such, his/her task is to bring together a number of issues, treated in an otherwise sectoral manner by the regional and departmental prefectoral services, under the common 'environmental' banner. Given the complexity of French territorial administration and government, one should not be surprised that the DIREN often find this a difficult task, made all the more so by the perceived lack of spatial and administrative coherence in environmental policy as a whole [*Deveze and Sanson, 1993*].

The Regions, Departments and the Municipalities

If, as Prieur [*1991: 220*] maintains, political decentralization ultimately did little to strengthen the limited environmental responsibilities of the regions, the departments and the municipalities did gain significantly. Both as a directly elected assembly and as a level of state administration (that is, both politically and administratively), the department has become a central focus for environmental policy-making within France. Formally, the legal responsibilities of the departments in the environmental field are limited to the management of sensitive natural areas, forest fire protection and the laying out and maintenance of long-distance footpaths. However, there is an important distinction to be made between these often regulatory functions and actual policy-making roles. The departments have been the principal beneficiaries of decentralization in general and, as environmental policy extends into virtually all other policy domains, their role here has become equally essential. Particularly important in this respect are the numerous consultative committees and departmental services which advise upon, elaborate and coordinate environmental actions within the department and officially comment upon pollution controls and authorizations (which legally remain the domain of the departmental prefect). The combination, at the departmental level of the elected *conseil général* and its services, essentially responsible for policy and finance, and the prefect and the prefectoral services, charged with legal control, regulation and authorization, makes for a formidable and effective level of environmental policy-making and implementation.

The municipality, as the basic unit of French local government, is also endowed, following political decentralization, with certain important environmental responsibilities. These fall readily into two broad domains, land-use planning and amenity control, though the former is by far and away the more important, constituting, it might be argued, one of the key elements of the entire decentralization process. All municipalities currently have the right to draw up local land-use plans. Although these plans must take all relevant legal steps to ensure the protection of the environment, they have subsequently emerged as fundamental tools in the local development process, because they free local municipal authorities from the generally restrictive nature of national planning rules and guidelines. This newly acquired freedom of action and the deregulation that has accompanied it has revealed both the positive and the negative aspects of decentralized local planning, particularly its application to environmental protection. Faced with domestic economic and political pressures, local politicians have frequently tended to ignore long-term environmental considerations in favour of shorter term economic benefits. Moreover, the municipality often anticipates state advice (particularly as this often takes a long time to appear), and many of the new-style local plans are effectively implemented without full legal (that is, state) control. Where infractions occur, they are either ignored, taken before the administrative tribunal or, ultimately referred to the *Conseil d'Etat.*

In order to avoid these irregularities, planning law is becoming noticeably more restrictive. This is also a way of reconciling local planning with greater respect for the environment. The Coastline Act of 3 January 1986, for instance, has become a key instrument in restraining the pro-development actions of municipal councils. The decree of application of 20 September 1989 laid down zones and natural areas that had to be protected by local plans and verified by the departmental or regional prefects. Here the state, as guarantor of environmental protection in the general public interest, has sought to take back some of the decision-making liberty initially offered to the municipalities in the euphoria of political decentralization.

The strengthening of municipal and departmental roles in environmental policy-making and the still limited powers of the regions in this domain, suggests that the latter are in danger of being left behind in the growing political and public concern for environmental issues. Indeed, a recent survey of DIREN directors revealed that none were satisfied with the current distribution of environmental responsibilities between the different tiers of local government and state administration [*Deveze and Sanson, 1993*]. The partnership roles of the regions may give them an important entry point into policy elaboration and implementation but, despite their seemingly key geographical position as federating structures, their anticipated role in drawing up broad schema, in coordinating local action and in providing a regional overview has, thus far, failed to emerge. In the following section, we examine the reasons for this failure.

THE REGIONS: AN EFFECTIVE LEVEL OF ENVIRONMENTAL POLICY-MAKING?

The environmental domain provides a valuable example of the manner in which decentralized institutions can be frustrated by political realities. Decentralization was announced as a new starting point: 'This government intends to break with this situation ... (centralization) ... It seeks to draw to a close this form of policy-making' claimed the initial declaration of the Bill concerning the separation of responsibilities. The reform of local government has been fundamental and far-reaching. From the point of view of the state, the power of the centre has been transferred to the periphery through the strengthening of the powers of the prefect. He/she becomes, amongst other things, uniquely responsible for the local field services of the state in a wide range of different areas (agriculture, planning, transport, among others). For the departments and municipalities, the gains are clear, particularly in the fields of land-use planning, amenity, finance and policy-making. The position of the regions remains, however, ill-defined and lacking a clear focus.

In their six or so years of existence as genuine components of French local government, the regions have sought to define a policy niche with respect to the environment, one that does not duplicate those more wide-ranging environmental policy functions handed over to other authorities under decentralization. Nonetheless, the regions remain only limited actors in local environmental policy-making. Functionally, they lack a defined policy role. In addition, they have been constrained by a set of institutional and policy limitations that stem from the existing division of responsibilities between regions and departments. It is clear that this division, laid down in the legislation of the early 1980s, continues to hinder the effective operation of regional government as a whole. As Gaussen [1992] argues: 'This feeling of incompleteness relates especially to continual flux in the division of powers across the territorial levels of government which are simultaneously very fragmented and autonomous'.

The constraints on developing an unambiguous role for the policy-making and administrative institutions at the regional level might be said to stem from three principal factors: the historical antecedents of regional level administration which, as we have identified above, have been consultative rather than decision oriented; the lack of specific interventionist and policy-making powers in the environmental domain; and the failed development of a complementary rather than competitive policy-making environment. All three factors have affected, we would argue, both regional government and the regional bureaux of the state concerned with the environment.

As indicated above, the principal functions of regional government in environmental matters are consultative and coordinative. Yet, to a certain extent, this mandate could be one of the region's strongest cards. Not only does it permit the bringing together of different regional services under (however temporarily erected) environmental banners, but it can also allow the regions to mediate between different communes and departments which might otherwise fail to arrive at a common standpoint. Thus, in Languedoc-Roussillon, the region, in association with the DRAE and later the DIREN, has played a key role in animating and bringing together different scientific and planning approaches to coastal management [*Conseil régional de Languedoc-Roussillon, 1988*]. Results from these studies have subsequently assisted the elaboration of both the *Contrat de Plan Etat-Région*, a regional responsibility, and the Coastline Management Plan, the responsibility of the regional level state services. This brokerage function, which is often pursued in association with state services and private research organizations, is, we maintain, a viable area for the development of a genuine regional input into environmental policy-making. That said, such opportunities tend to exist only in specific policy domains, notably water management, and certain territorial sectors, notably coastlines where the need for an integrated, coherent policy rarely translates into political will on the part of neighbouring local administrations. Furthermore, success is often linked, at least in the eyes of participating communes and departments, to the financial recompense that regional intervention can bring.

A second limitation to regional efficacy stems from their relative lack of specific interventionist and regulatory powers. This was particularly evident in the first attempts to establish a viable regional-level environmental administration. The *Délégués régionaux à l'Architecture et à l'Environnement* (DRAE), forerunners to the DIREN, were created in 1979 and replaced in 1991. Their somewhat eclectic remit included the protection of natural and historic sites, the promotion of good planning and architectural design and, through consultation and advice, the adoption of sound environmental protection measures in other local policies. Only in the first of these were the DRAE given any real regulatory powers. For the others, they performed an essentially consultative and advisory function; actual policy decisions were taken and implemented at the departmental and even municipal levels, while regulatory policies were determined by the state. As a result of their vague legal status, inadequate resources, powers and authority and their essentially alien profile with respect to established local politico-administrative structures [*Romi, 1990*], the DRAE were never able to establish themselves either as effective local representatives of their parent ministry (Environment), or as effective agents of environmental policy. Indeed, at the departmental level they were marginalized not only by their own weaknesses, but also by the growing policy-making strengths of the individual departments.

The failure of the DRAE to emerge as either powerful or relevant environmental policy actors was in part a function of their administrative context. It was also however, a reflection of the continued ambiguity surrounding the purpose of a regional tier of either local government or state administration in the environmental policy domain. Environmental policy is a continually shifting balance of regulatory control and negotiation which cannot be disassociated from all other areas of social and economic life. As decentralization has handed power for the management of these other areas to the departments and communes, the presence of a regional environmental policy structure seems increasingly anachronistic other than in the context of very specific territorial actions. Furthermore, there has been a clear contradiction between the effective deregulation of land-use planning powers following decentralization (under which mayors of municipalities have an almost free hand in selecting development options), and the often expressed desire to maintain, at the regional level, a broad and coordinating function. Thus, while the 1980s saw a veritable explosion of local land-use planning and development control documents, broader sub-regional planning virtually disappeared [*Vasselin, 1991*]. Land-use planning, in what has undoubtedly become one of the more severe unintended consequences of decentralization, has become highly localized and, in many cases uncoordinated. This, coupled with the often scant attention paid to the environmental consequences of development, has made the regions' role in promoting and encouraging environmental planning extremely arduous.

A third factor limiting the effectiveness of French regions in environmental policy-making derives from the political and administrative complexity surrounding decentralization [*Hertzog, 1993*] and the subsequent division of powers and legal competencies, particularly in the environmental domain. This necessitates, virtually by definition, a cooperative and transversal approach to policy-making. For harmony to exist between the various components of French central and territorial government and administration, particularly at the level of the departments, (the major beneficiaries of decentralization), a genuine dialogue is needed between elected local government councillors, keen to flex their new political muscles, and the state. Whilst the latter is always in a strong position as a result of its *a posteriori* administrative control over local authority actions, it is weak in terms of policy-making and financial competencies. The transfer of important policy-making powers to local government in the early 1980s has upset the hierarchy of political power, despite the fact that the prefect continues to have precedence over the president of the departmental or regional council. For the state, decentralization has altered neither the elected representatives nor the civil servants and the relationship between the two remains as complex as ever.

Neither has decentralization resolved the fundamental difficulty surrounding environmental policy-making; how to establish an administrative or policy-making apparatus capable of dealing with an inherently transversal issue, the environment, within a rigidly segmented and hierarchical policy-making structure? For local councillors and state servants, decentralization has ultimately had little effect upon the technocratic conception of, and vertical and sectoral approaches towards, societal issues. Moreover, in bringing policy-making power closer to the citizen, decentralization has made the policy-making task even more complex. Confronted with the needs and opinions of their electorate, neither local councillors nor representatives of the state can afford to act alone. Increasingly, a wide range of policies require the taking into account of local political circumstances as well as national interests and regulations. Furthermore, the issues addressed, when they are dealt with at the local level, are inexorably bound up with the local society and therefore respond badly to simple partial or sectoral treatments.

The decentralization reforms assumed the creation of a local partnership between politicians and officials, but did not insist upon it. Predictably, and in keeping with French administrative tradition, all of the relevant actors have subsequently sought to define their own specific areas of action and to position themselves advantageously with respect to forces of dependency or independence. Thus, at the departmental level, a number of former state bureaux, such as those dealing with agriculture, health and planning, have been divided in two (the legal term being 'partitioned'). One part, which deals with regulation and legal control remains under state tutelage, whilst the other part, which is involved in policy-making and, increasingly, programme financing, has handed over to the departments. This division should have ended all the tensions arising from the ambivalent post-decentralization status of these bureaux as state services placed at the disposition of the department (or the region in certain cases). However, for the moment at least, this administrative surgery has had anything but a therapeutic effect. In reality, the state and the department rely firmly and solely upon the competencies of their own services though, as originally envisaged, the two should be complementary and their actions interlinked. The environment, potentially a major beneficiary of this complementarity, has thus become a highly fragmented political and administrative domain. The legislation leaves local government completely free to organize itself as it wishes. The difficulty of establishing a genuine dialogue and partnership between local government and state services with respect to environmental issues is today a real problem – the environment being so tentacular an issue. The state is entrenched in its regulatory functions, the department in its desire to express its policy-making liberty. If an issue is particularly controversial, the political scene takes on the image of gang warfare.

A sort of cultural revolution of local administration is underway. Faced with the flexibility of local government organization, even local state services are seeking to break the sectoral mould of environmental policy and regulatory responses. In 15 departments, the state bureaux for agriculture (DDAF) and land-use planning (DDE) are experimenting with closer collaboration. This has been particularly successful where environmental issues are concerned, particularly those associated with water. This approach could be adopted more generally in the creation of an inter-service organization at the departmental level of state bureaux, responsible for water, leading to the elaboration of integrated management structures. Such an approach has already been adopted with respect to land use management. However, to be really effective at the local level, this opening up of state services must be accompanied by the development of local partnership.

CONCLUSION: THE FUTURE OF THE FRENCH REGIONS

The position of the region within the territorial balance of France has recently emerged as a key issue on the contemporary political agenda. The current debate concerning the organization and planning of the French territorial space and the continuing economic and demographic dominance of the Paris region have thrown discussions of regional roles and functions once more into the political arena. The responsibilities handed over to the regions during the decentralization process have made this level of administration and government a focus for current political attention and concern. What then, are likely to be the central areas of regional intervention in the future? We believe that French regions will emerge as key actors at two levels; first at the interface between the locality and the European Union; secondly, as coordinating partners in the growing area of contractual developmental and environmental programmes at the local level.

A European Role

Within the framework of Europe, the region is beginning to appear as a key territorial unit, economically viable in its own right and of a more appropriate size within a supra-national territory. Although, in comparison with other 'Euro-regions', French regions are comparatively small [*Labasse, 1991*], the political development of the European Union is undoubtedly reinforcing both the political and legal status of the French and other regions [*Pujol, 1993*] and, indeed, their public profile [*Directorate General for Regional Policies, 1993*]. Clearly, with increasing European integration, a regional tier of government becomes ever more relevant [*Pujol, 1992*] even though this might, in the future, necessitate the regrouping of certain regions [*Némery, 1993*]. The distance between Brussels and the Commission on the one hand, and the individual units of local governments, on the other, is regarded as too great for effective dialogue. Hence many regional authorities were among the first to seek and express a European voice. They are now emerging as key interlocutors as evinced by the Maastricht Treaty's inclusion of the establishment of a consultative European Union Committee of the Regions. Furthermore, regions would appear to be, to a certain extent, the natural beneficiaries of the principle of subsidiarity, which seeks to place policy-making and regulatory functions at the most appropriate sub-Union level within individual Member states.

For the moment, however, French regions are still hampered by fragmented structures and administrations which have the effect of blocking and restraining regional development and economic stimulation initiatives. These practical difficulties are well illustrated by the attempts of the frontier regions, Alsace and Languedoc-Roussillon, to establish cooperative relationships with neighbouring regions in Germany and Spain. While, the German Land of Baden-Württemberg is a highly organized regional entity endowed with autonomous government and considerable independence in a variety of policy domains, the French Alsace region combines two departments, four Chambers of Commerce and a panoply of often complicated administrative and governmental interrelationships, all of which have similarly complex links with Paris. Nonetheless, French frontier regions, despite their limitations compared with their foreign counterparts, are emerging as an example to be followed by others. Throughout France, individual regions are increasingly seeking to shed the heavy administrative structures inherited from their past in order to become viable and efficient organisms for planning, spatial management and economic development within both a national and European context.

Understandably, French regions have not been allowed to play the European card unchallenged. Individual departments, if not negotiating directly with the Commission are also seeking an independent lobbying profile at Brussels. Thus, the obligation to pass through the region in negotiating FEDER aid may become just that, an obligation with little real policy-making substance behind it. Finally, the French delegation to the Committee of the Regions will comprise representatives from departments and municipalities as well as from the regions; a '*réprésentation équitable*' in the words of the Secretary of State for Local Government [*Sueur, 1992*], which might further erode the standing of the French regions. Even so, given the size of the European Union, it seems likely that it will be the regions, rather than the departments, which will emerge, in some form or other, as de Tocqueville's '*corps intermediaries*' between super-state and locality. The real threat to this regional renaissance will come, not from other levels of local government, but from the larger urban centres, the self-defined 'city regions'. Where a region is dominated by one major urban centre, which demands a distinct voice in regional planning and in regional representation, there is considerable room for conflicting spatial and economic goals to emerge (see chapters by Balme and Le Galès in this issue). Where such conflicts arise, it is by no means the case that the regional interest will necessarily prevail. Within the European Union, this 'metropolitanization' is not exclusive to France [*Biarez, 1993*]. Moreover, the relative political weakness of French regions inhibits the formulation of coherent planning schema. The political (and economic) importance of the city of Lyon, within the region of Rhône-Alpes, is a good case in point, bearing witness to the potential conflicts of interest between the goals of the regional assembly and those of a large town.

A Territorial Role

A second area where regional government and administration is showing a developing competence, is again one for which it would seem to be ideally suited. If the years immediately following decentralization were marked by a rampant territorial individualism, a more recent trend has been towards increased local cooperation. Although intermunicipal structures date from the 1970s, the rapid growth of intermunicipal approaches in planning, service provision and development has been one of the most widely observed phenomenon of the late 1980s and early 1990s. Entirely voluntary (no government would risk enforcing municipal regrouping), inter-communal and even intercantonal structures are becoming virtually the norm in an increasingly wide range of policy domains. Furthermore, following the Law of 6 February 1992, they are actively encouraged by the state which offers certain types of intermunicipal structures extensive policy-making responsibilities, particularly in the fields of land-use planning and economic development, and a degree of financial autonomy, through the ability to levy specific local taxes. This drive towards composite structures, with all the political mediation, participation and discussion that this entails, is in a sense contrary to the logic hitherto pursued by individual municipalities and also departments in their search for autonomy and independence. The new model or political 'style' is one that favours cooperation and coordination, negotiation and contractual financing. These characteristics are more similar to those of the region than the department. It is not surprising therefore, that regions are emerging as major partners in the process of intermunicipal amalgamation. On the one hand, they both finance directly and channel state finance towards intermunicipal groupings, thereby becoming contractual partners in the development and planning process, as well as in environmental protection schemes. On the other hand, they genuinely coordinate intermunicipal actions, a brokerage role for which they have long been rehearsing. Of course, contractual programmes do not have to pass by the region. Indeed, the multiplicity of contracts established between individual towns and the central state suggest again that 'city regions' are perhaps the greatest challenge to the justification of a regional tier. Nevertheless, many local intermunicipal groupings believe they can negotiate better with the region than with the department, the more traditional coordinator of cooperative development programmes. Thus, the development of intermunicipal groups, it is suggested here, is closer in spirit and rationale to regionalization than to decentralization.

A Continuing Debate

The growing presence of the regions on the French political stage, supported by the expanding cast of intercommunal and intercantonal actors, has recently led the state to reaffirm the presence of the department. One needs to remember that the powers of the state at the local level, in the form of the departmental and regional prefects and their respective services, were widely seen as being considerably weakened by the process of decentralization. Logically, therefore, any growth in the political strength and representational legitimacy of the regions will, almost inevitably, lead to an associated increase in the state's presence at the regional level. The implication of this is that the state's representatives and services at the departmental level will see their power concomitantly weakened. Legally, there is no hierarchical relationship between the state's regional and departmental services, with civil servants from both being considered equal. In practice, however, any change in the delicate balance of responsibilities between the two is likely to have significant repercussions amongst the *grands corps* of the French civil service who make up the state's presence at these different levels. Already losers (in some respects) in the process of decentralization, civil servants are unwilling to accept further constraints on their career profiles. Thus, while proclaiming a renewed commitment to regional planning and economic development, founded upon an increased political profile for the regions, the government is, at the same time, reaffirming the place of the departments as the guarantors of local political, social and administrative coherence. The senior civil service, a major power within French administration, is home to the centralizing force of the state. It is unlikely therefore that, in the near future, regional political intervention will be given a totally free rein. As the youngest elements of local government, the regions are perhaps the most expendable [*Hertzog, 1993*].

Yet France with its historic and perhaps impracticable emphasis upon the lower tiers of territorial administration (notably the 36, 433 communes), needs, in the context of Europe, a level of government and administration capable of linking the supranational level to the locality. The regions have, at the very least, the geographical extent and the negotiating capacity required.

REFERENCES

Biarez, S., 1993, 'Ville, Région, Etat, le dialogue en Europe', in J-V. Némery and S. Wachter (eds), *Entre l'Europe et la Décentralisation* (Paris: Editions de l'Aube).

Blumann, C., 1989, 'La prise en compte de la politique régionale et de la politique de l'environnement dans les autres politiques communautaires', in M. Prieur (ed.), *Europe des régions et l'environnement* (Limoges: Presses Universitaires de France).

Bodiguel, M. ,1991, 'La France', in M. Bodiguel (ed.), *Produire et Préserver l'Environnement*, (Paris: l'Harmattan).

Buller, H., 1992, 'Agriculture and Environment in Western Europe', in K. Hoggart (ed.), *Agricultural Change, Environment and Economy* (London: Mansell).

Capul, J-Y., 1985, 'La région et la décentralisation' in *La Décentralisation en Marche,* Cahiers Français, No. 220, (Paris: La Documentation française).

Conseil régional de Basse Normandie, 1991, *Le Plan régional 1994-1998* (Caen).

Conseil régional de Languedoc-Roussillon, 1988, *Les espaces lagunaires du Languedoc-Roussillon* (Montpellier).

Deveze, J. and C. Sanson, 1993, 'Répartition des compétences entre l'Etat et les collectivités territoriales: le point de vue des DIREN', *Aménagement et Nature*, 110, pp.2-4.

Directorate General for Regional Policies, 1993, *No Europe without its regions* (Brussels: Eurobarometer, INRA).

Gaussen, F., 1992, 'Les Régions et l'Etat', *Le Monde*, 6 March 1992.

Hertzog, R., 1993, 'Les responsabilités des administrations locales', 41-60 in J-V. Némery and S. Wachter (eds), *Entre l'Europe et la Décentralisation* (Paris: Editions de l'Aube).

Labasse, J., 1991, *L'Europe des Régions* (Paris: Flammarion).

Logié, G., 1992, *La Coopération intercommunale en milieu rural* (Paris: Syros Alternatives).

Morand-Deviller, J., 1987, *Le Droit de l'Environnement* (Paris: PUF).

Némery, J-C., 1993, 'Les institutions territoriales françaises à l'épreuve de l'Europe', in J-V. Némery and S. Wachter (eds), *Entre l'Europe et la Décentralisation* (Paris: Editions de l'Aube).

Prieur, M., 1988, 'La répartition des compétences entre la CEE, les Etats et les collectivités locales en matièrede l'Environnement', in J. Charpentier (ed.), *La protection de l'Environnement par les Communautés Européennes*.

Prieur, M., 1991, *Droit de l'Environnement* (Paris: Dalloz).

Poujade, R., 1975, *Le ministère de l'impossible* (Paris: Calman-Lévy).

Pouvoirs, 1992, Edition spéciale, *La décentralisation*.

Pujol, J., 1992, 'Les régions et l'Europe', *Le Monde*, 21 September 1992.

Pujol, J., 1993, 'Vers une Europe des régions?', *L'Evènement Européen*, 21, pp.83-94.

Romi, R., 1990, *L'administration de l'environnement* (Paris: Erasme).

Sueur, J-P., 1992, Quoted in *Le Monde*, 19 October 1992.

Vasselin, L., 1991, 'La relance des schémas directeurs', *Etudes foncières*, 50, pp.20-23.

The Status of Maritime and Insular France: The DOM-TOM and Corsica

HELEN HINTJENS, JOHN LOUGHLIN
and CLAUDE OLIVESI

INTRODUCTION: THE DIVERSITY OF OVERSEAS FRANCE AND THE CONTEXT OF REFORM

Today, overseas France (*la France d'Outre-mer*) consists of the remains of the French colonial Empire, what Claude Guillebaud termed the 'confetti of Empire'. These territories have also been termed the 'debris of Empire', with the implication that their time has passed; they are anachronisms in an era of independence. For different reasons, these mostly tiny pieces of territory chose, between 1958 and 1962, not to separate themselves from the *mère patrie*, but to remain integrated or closely associated with France. This article sketches the constitutional picture of this dispersed ensemble, but focuses on the recent experience of regional reforms in the four overseas departments of Guadeloupe, French Guiana, Martinique and Réunion in particular. However, included in this section is the island of Corsica which, although it has been traditionally regarded as part of 'metropolitan' France, exhibits certain characteristics, deriving largely from it being an island, which make it similar to the overseas territories in many respects. Moreover, recent attempts at providing Corsica with a special statute have, in fact, brought it constitutionally closer to the more traditional overseas territories.

The overseas reality of France has been strongly influenced by its colonial history. However, maritime France, as these territories are sometimes called, has been subject to ten years of regional and institutional reforms, engineered from above, and taking place in a context of a shrinking national budget devoted to the DOM-TOM (*départements et territoires d'outre-mer*). According to Albrechts [1989: 4], regional reforms have come in response to the widespread 'failure of the state'. There is a widely perceived need to find alternative means of formulating and implementing policies which could be more relevant and 'effective in the contemporary French context than the central planning of the 1960s and 1970s could be. As in the case of Corsica, these regional reforms have also been introduced in response to demands for greater local autonomy from the electorate and politicians within DOM-TOM and Corsica [*Loughlin, 1989*]. Territorially-based claims for more devolved economic and administrative policy-making have sometimes also overlapped with language-based claims to a distinct regional identity and special provisions in the media, and in education and cultural life.

THE DOM-TOM

In trying to understand in depth this unusual contemporary reality, one soon becomes aware of the great diversity of what are called the DOM-TOM. They by no means form an homogeneous whole. The term DOM-TOM itself reflects some complex categorizations which date from the colonial period, and as Jacques Ziller argues, 'The overseas departments and territories, far from being members of a single family, are distinct in almost every respect, except that they form the last remains of the French colonial Empire' [*1991: 15*].

Without wishing to retell French colonial history, it would be useful to recall a number of factors that have influenced the present-day nature of these parts of the French Republic. France's colonial problem was felt at its most acute during the period of the Fourth Republic after the Second World War. The Brazzaville Conference (30 January–8 February 1944) had tried, albeit with some ambivalence, to meet the aspirations for sovereignty of those peoples of the Empire who had shown solidarity with Free France. De Gaulle addressed the possible evolution of these aspirations in the following terms:

> In French Africa, as in all the lands where people live under the protection of our flag, no progress would be possible unless men, in the country of their birth, did not benefit materially and morally from it; if they could not raise themselves up, bit by bit, to the level where they would become able to take part in the management of their own affairs. The duty of France is to see that this should come about [*1970*].

The Fourth Republic would indeed have to face several colonial problems (Madagascar, Indochina and North Africa). However, the key set of events of this period was the Algerian crisis which began on 1 November 1954 and which was to have profound consequences on the political life of metropolitan France. As a result of this crisis, De Gaulle came to power in 1958 and the Gaullist régime was forced to redefine the relations between France and the different parts of the Empire. During his investiture speech, De Gaulle pronounced that his principal objective would be to present to the French people a new form of relationship between France and 'the peoples which are associated with it'.[1]

Overview of the Constitutional Evolution of the DOM-TOM

Which overseas 'peoples' would be affected by this 'reorganization'? In the first place, there were those found in the *départements d'outre-mer* (DOM). This term first appeared in the French political and juridical lexicon in Article 27 of the Constitution of 27 October 1946. This gave a constitutional status to the famous law of 19 March 1946 which had turned the *vieilles colonies* of Martinique, Guadeloupe, French Guiana and Reunion into fully-fledged French departments. Because of the length of time they had been occupied by France and because of their privileged relation with the '*metropole*' (mainland France), the people of these four 'old colonies' were seen as fully assimilable in ways that the people of associated colonial territories were not. They were also small in terms of population (see Table 7:1).

The move to integrate these colonies was the result of local demands: in this case of demands made by the representatives of the local populations (including the then communist deputy of Fort de France, Aimé Césaire). The provision governing the DOM became Article 73 of the 1958 Constitution. 53 years later, Césaire gave the following reasons for this original request: 'the people ... wanted to move from the system of rule by decree to the rule of law; they wanted their dignity, and greater solidarity from metropolitan France, and they wanted the introduction of social and welfare legislation ...' (*Le Monde*, 12 April 1994).

Maritime France also includes the TOM. As was the case for the DOM, the creation of this category was the result of the situation after the Second World War and appeared in the Constitution of the Fourth Republic. At that time, the TOM comprised French colonies which were mostly in Africa. During the constitutional referendum of 28 September 1958 they were given two options: to stay within the French Republic or to become independent. Only Guinea under Seke Toure chose the latter option, and on 30 September France renounced its sovereignty over it.

For the territories which had chosen to remain within the French Republic, there were three possibilities open to them under article 76 of the new Constitution: to keep the status of TOM as defined by article 74c; to adopt the status of Member State of the French Community, or to become a DOM. It should be noted that these three options accorded closely with the three alternatives to colonial status, as specified by the United Nations, namely: free association with an independent state; full independence; and voluntary integration into an independent state.

The TOM was an administrative organization, a type of *collectivité territoriale*, as were the municipalities and departments. In effect, the referendum on status functioned as a kind of 'sieve' which allowed the

TABLE 7:1
POPULATION OF THE FRENCH REPUBLIC, FRENCH CAMEROUNS
AND TOGO IN 1958

Algeria (including Sahara)			9,500,00
DOM	La Réunion	274,000	
	Martinique	239,000	
	Guadeloupe	229,000	
	Guyane	27,000	
Total (DOM):			769,000
French West			
Africa:	Sénégal	2,000,000	
	Mauritanie	600,00	
	Soudan	3,700,000	
	Haute Volta	3,220,000	
	Guinee	2,490,000	
	Cote d'Ivoire	2,480,000	
	Dahomey (Bénin)	1,700,000	
	Niger	2,410,000	
Total (FWA):			18,600,000
French Central			
Africa:	Gabon	410,000	
	Moyen Congo	700,000	
	Oubangui	1,100,000	
	Tchad	2,300,000	
Total (FCA):			4,510,000
Madagasca			4,500,000
Comores			170,000
Somalis			65,000
Saint Pierre et Miquelon			4,500
Polynésie Française			75,000
Nouvelle Caledonie			65,000
Total of French Overseas Territories			**38,258,500**
Togo			1,050,000
Cameroun			3,100,000
TOTAL of the overseas population represented in the Federative Assembly			**42,408,500**
METROPOLITAN FRANCE			**44,000,000**

Source: Documents pour servir à l'histoire de l'élaboration de la Constitution du 4 Octobre 1958, vol. 1, p.576; Comité National chargé de la publication des travaux préparatoires des institutions de la Vème République: La Documentation Français, trimestre 1, 1987.

peoples of these territories to decide on the intensity of their relations with the Republic. The status of TOM left considerable room for manoeuvre in this respect; the people of a particular TOM could either weaken the links with France, to the point of separation, or they could strengthen them to the point of complete departmental assimilation.

The intrinsically evolutionary character of the TOM organizes them according to the principle of 'legislative specificity' under Article 74c of the Constitution. This allows the legislator to depart from the norm with regard to the institutional organization of local authorities; to exclude the application of French law, except where the TOM are explicitly mentioned; and requires the territorial assemblies of the TOM to be involved in advance in matters that affect their constituents. 'All these elements contribute to a diversification of the status of the overseas territories, both in form and content' [*Ziller, 1991*]. This leads to a conception of 'internal autonomy' which takes into account the 'indivisibility' of the Republic and national sovereignty (Article 3c).

Following consultations with their territorial assemblies, five entities with small populations and tiny territories chose the TOM option: the Comoro Islands, French Somalia, New Caledonia, French Polynesia, and the archipelago of St-Pierre et Miquelon. Wallis and Futuna joined the group after a decision of its assembly on 27 December 1959. In the same year, the African TOM and Madagascar became Member States of the new Community. However, the Community disappeared almost as soon as it was set up because several of its members became independent at the beginning of the 1960s. It is worth noting that at this point, none of the territories or member states chose to become a DOM.

Today there are only three TOM: New Caledonia, Polynesia and Wallis and Futuna, all three located in the Pacific region. The Comoro Islands and French Somalia become independent states on 31 December 1975 and 27 June 1977 respectively. Compared with the provisions of regional reforms in the DOM, the recent evolution of the status of French Polynesia and New Caledonia is in some respects enviable in the powers accorded local assemblies. Strict limits have been imposed on the decentralization reforms in the DOM by the decision of the Conseil Constitutionnel that a single assembly would be unconstitutional.

For some time, St Pierre et Miquelon, two small islands located off the coast of Canada, had DOM status (under the law of 19 July 1976), but in 1985 (by the law of 11 June) the islands became a *collectivité territoriale*, a territorial administrative entity that is neither DOM nor TOM, but somewhere in between and 'sui generis'. This formula represents a legislative innovation, combining elements of legislation applicable to both DOM and TOM, and first appeared in the island of Mayotte. As part of the archipelagic TOM of the Comoro Islands, the population of Mayotte overwhelmingly rejected independence in a referendum on 22 December 1974. Subsequently, the population of the island also refused TOM status (in a referendum of 11 April 1976), and this led Parliament to create a new territorial status for the island, on the basis of Articles 72 and 34 of the Constitution. As *collectivités territoriales*, however, the status of Mayotte and of St Pierre et Miquelon remains in suspense.

Finally, this intermediate 'category', eclectic in nature, has gained a third entity: Corsica (see below). This island was given its own *Statut Particulier* by the law of 2 March 1982, but has become a *collectivité territoriale de la République*, with specific powers and institutions (law no. 91-428 of 13 May 1991).

Unlike the TOM, the DOM are just a specific category of territorial authority. Their institutional organization and their powers are very similar to those of metropolitan departments. But the huge distance separating them from the '*metropole*' and the delicate balance of their social and cultural characteristics have meant that they enjoy a number of legislative features designed to preserve their specificity, and to ensure that they are not unduly disadvantaged.

Regional Reform and Local Politics in the DOM

Formal structures are more or less identical in the four DOM, but this has not prevented a process of fragmentation from taking place during more than a decade of regional reforms and decentralization measures. Since 1981, political life in Guadeloupe, Martinique, French Guiana and Reunion has become increasingly inward-looking. The departmentalist option came to be challenged by a part of public opinion and by some political groups in the DOM at the start of the 1960s. 'Assimilationist' departmentalization policies were thought to be incapable of resolving the particular problems of these territories, since no matter how much account was taken of their geographical and economic handicaps, colonial-type structures remained alongside a new and 'artificial' type of economic development, which was seen to bring little gain to the local people.

The French state has indeed been singularly unsuccessful in its planning efforts in the overseas departments. Their economies have become hybrids, classic 'dualistic' case-studies. The same could be said of the economies of the TOM; but in their case, the results of economic policies do not have the same direct consequences for centre-periphery relations, since there is much greater local autonomy and a local legislative assembly. It has proved particularly difficult to attract capital investment into the DOM, in spite of a policy of 'defiscalization' introduced in the early 1980s. In part, this reflects the very success of departmental policies in improving wages, social security cover and other provisions for workers in the DOM. Any proposal to reduce the level of social security cover or wages in order to encourage investment has resulted in strikes and protests in the DOM (as in 1986 when Jacques Chirac made such a proposal).

On the other hand, special intervention is demanded by many political representatives of the DOM to compensate for these regions' particular handicaps of location, history, demography and small size. Subsidies for transport, special taxation powers, preferential markets for exports and production subsidies all continue to be called for, although such special measures may be threatened by the advent of the European Union. Such policies enable unprofitable activities to continue, and constitute a form of subsidized job-creation in departments with the highest unemployment levels in France.

Unemployment has nonetheless continued to rise in each of the DOM. Rising expectations have resulted from the regional reforms which, as Charles Gore has observed '... can have the *unintentional* effect of mobilizing political groups which demand more resources and rights for 'their' region' [*Gore, 1984: 262*].

Civil servants in the DOM have traditionally received a premium of between 40 and 70 per cent of their salaries simply for working overseas. The *Rapport Ripert* of 1989 recommended that such premiums should be removed. Any attempt to do so, however, has resulted in strikes and vocal opposition from public sector employees; in 1991 such strikes were called in all four departments (*Le Monde*, 16 March 1991). Local businesses supported the civil servants, fearing a loss in their trade as result of such cuts.

Before 1982, the main challenge to the French state's legitimacy in the overseas departments came from the left and the autonomist and pro-independence parties. For a time, regionalization appeared to satisfy these groups in their desire for greater control over the levers of power. With time, the impact of regional reform has become more complex. Ironically, the emergence of localized forms of political discourse and practice (for example, left-right electoral alliances on regional issues) has occurred at a time when public opinion in metropolitan France has become more indifferent than ever to the future status of the DOM within the Republic [*Lacoste, 1991: 12*]. The fear of abandonment is as strong among the electorate as the desire for greater local autonomy and control over policy.

Regionalization has not resolved the question of these departments' future status, a status which may appear increasingly anachronistic at a time when the borders between continental western Europe and the rest of the world are hardening in the context of a 'fortress Europe'.

These problems are far from having been resolved in the 1990s, in spite of the efforts of local regional institutions, central government and the EU, which has introduced special regional plans for each DOM. Regionalization has formally replaced the DOM-region's dependence on the central planning institutions and ministries in Paris with so-called 'contract-plans' agreed between the state, the region and the department. In practice, however, the ability to redistribute resources - what has sometimes been called 'stomach politics' - remains the essential means of operation at the regional, departmental and municipal levels [*Constant, 1988: 129-140*]. This strategy of legitimation may be threatened by the budgetary cuts being imposed on overseas as well as in metropolitan France. In the current environment, the overseas regions must compete, in a zero-sum fashion, for resources from the centre. This adds to an underlying sense of insecurity about the permanence of their present political status as integral parts of the French Republic and the European Union.

A recent study by the overseas (DOM-TOM) group for the XIth Plan confirmed this diagnosis and emphasized the seriousness of the situation in the DOM (as well as in the TOM):

> More or less the same few political representatives always take part in debates on the budget of overseas (France), and after voicing some disquiet, they may obtain some favours for their own constituencies. In these localities, the people's impoverishment ... is administered by overpaid officials who write abstract reports, who are joined from time to time by expensive units of the special security police (CRS) (*Regards sur l'Actualité*).

The possibilities of financial corruption may even have increased as a result of decentralization and seem to have tempted some elected politicians. That this situation has continued unchanged is the most likely explanation as to why a strong autonomist movement which subsequently changed into a separatist movement has developed since the 1980s.

This lack of political attention to the problems of the overseas territories led to the presentation of a list of electoral candidates described as the *Rassemblement de l'Outre-Mer et des Minorités* during the European elections of June 1994. This list was headed by Ernest Moutassamy, a deputy for Guadeloupe who was formerly associated with the Communist Party of Guadeloupe. The debate has oscillated between two contradictory positions: those who desire 'assimilation', and those who seek greater recognition of the specificity of the overseas territories in the form of a special legal status, specific politico-administrative institutions, extra powers in the economic and cultural domains, and ultimately in the granting of full independence and sovereignty.

Those who demand greater autonomy or independence also point to what they consider to be the negative consequences of European integration. In particular, they express concern at the implications for the DOM economies of the removal of subsidies and special taxes on imports. There is little doubt that these developments will have important consequences for the overseas territories, and many would agree with Edouard Glissant that '[t]he revision of relations with France is inevitable. Simple appearances are no longer enough' (*Le Monde*, 4 February 1994). The same opinion is also held by Aimé Césaire, when he argues that what is needed is '... to find a new framework, a new [legal] status that would enable us to remain within the French ensemble whilst also allowing us to be ourselves' (*Le Monde*, 12 April 1994).

Regionalist demands in the Caribbean, French Guiana and Reunion, based nominally on the distinctive 'creole' culture and character of these societies, have always been predicated on an increased transfer of resources towards the periphery rather than the reverse. Yet decentralization implies the shifting of responsibility for raising revenue to the local regional authorities. 'From now on, local-level solidarity must be added to national solidarity, and its acceptance can be seen as a test of the local will to develop' [*CGP, 1983: 103*]. 'Participation' is the order of the day; no-one is to wait for the state to deliver economic development; it is to come from the efforts of local people [*Hintjens, 1991*].

Creole Politics and Diverging Regional Identities

An interesting feature of intellectual life in Martinique and Guadeloupe in particular has been the shift from *négritude* as an alternative basis for identity to *créolite*. Starting with the work of Edouard Glissant, ideas of *antillanité* and a complex and composite creole identity have been taken further by writers like Daniel Maximin, Patrick Chamoiseau and Raphael Confiant, who express a new confidence in the assimilatory capacity of creole cultural life (*Le Monde*, 19 May 1990; *Libération*, 24 July 1989). If French identity is defined in terms of language, there can be considerable common ground. If it to be redefined, as the right would wish, on the basis of ethnicity or 'race', then there can be no common ground on which to reconstruct an Antillean identity within France.

The explicit embracing of cultural and familial mixity in the notion of *créolite* is seen by many as a breath of fresh air in the increasingly exclusionist mood of political rhetoric in metropolitan France and the rest of Europe. Like the rest of the DOM, however, the Antilles appear to be regarded as more outside than inside the Republic. Their overseas location, the colour of the people who originate from there, and their colonial history mark these departments out as different from the norm. In French public opinion, whilst the TOM are perceived as colonies, the DOM are located somewhere between 'France' and 'not-France'; that, after all, is clearly the meaning of the expression 'overseas France'.

In French Guiana, the creole population has declined from 75 to less than 40 per cent of the total population since 1970. This has been mainly due to immigration from surrounding countries, and the response from creole politicians and voters has been a tighter delineation of who is a Guyanese creole and who is not [*Jolivet, 1990*]. The autonomy granted to the local authorities in Guiana has been exceptional in several respects, and in particular in matters of immigration control. Measures have been taken that would not be permitted on the French mainland, including the expulsion of Surinamese refugees under conditions that led to objections from the United Nations High Commission on Refugees (*Le Figaro*, 9 April 1990; *Le Monde*, 9 July 1991). Recent political changes in French Guiana do not support the idea that there is any necessary connection between decentralization and the respect of human rights [*Lacoste, 1991: 18-19*].

There was a lull in pro-independence activity in Guadeloupe in the aftermath of the devastation caused by Hurricane Hugo in 1989. The main pro-independence party, the *Union pour la Libération de la Guadeloupe* renounced its demand of immediate sovereignty, and opted instead for something called 'associated independence' (*Le Monde*, 28 March 1990). Social unrest was also stalled by the Gulf War in 1991 (*Le Monde*, 29 January 1991). The issue of political reform has not disappeared off the agenda in the Antilles, however. In Martinique, the following year, there was a massive 22 per cent vote for the pro-independence parties immediately following another serious hurricane. The share of votes for the pro-independence party had grown from 4.5 per cent in 1983 and eight per cent in 1986 (*Le Monde*, 17 October 1990).

Reunion is a very distinctive overseas region in that it has no pro-independence movement of any significance. Unemployment is around 40 per cent, higher than in the Antilles or French Guiana. Reunion also absorbs fully one tenth of the national budget for the RMI (*Revenu Minimum d'Insertion* – a guaranteed minimum income), although it has only one per cent of the national population [*Catteau, 1992*]. In 1991, the island witnessed the first serious riots in recent history, when a local pirate television station, significantly named Tele Free-DOM, was closed down by the French national audio-visual authorities. This decision to close the only television station which broadcast in creole, prompted angry demonstrations which led to looting of supermarkets and car showrooms [*Chane-Kune, 1991*]. Deaths resulted from a fire in a looted shop, and representatives of the rioters subsequently put a list of 50 demands to the Minister of the DOM-TOM. None of these demands were even remotely separatist or pro-independence.

Jacques Vergès, acting as lawyer for the owner of Tele Free-DOM, Camille Sudre, argued that the Reunionnese who had rioted had done so because of the colonialist attitude of the audio-visual council in closing the station down. Their demands were for jobs (most of them were young unemployed men), for equal treatment and the right to use creole on the media (*Quotidien de Paris*, 7 March 1991). In 1992, Camille Sudre was elected chairman of the regional council, with 31 per cent of the vote going to his 'Free-DOM' list, much to the surprise of local politicians and the national press (*Le Quotidien de Paris*, 8 June 1992). Sudre's policies, whilst markedly creolist (in spite of his being metropolitan himself), are also integrationist. Among his demands, for example, is the request that the French government reintroduce free travel for migrants from Reunion seeking work in metropolitan France. The knock-on effects of events in New Caledonia, combined with the resurgence of metropolitan isolationism are greatly feared in Reunion.

An interesting outcome of the regionalization process has been the attempt by the French government, and the Ministry of the DOM-TOM in particular, to reintegrate the DOM – and the TOM – into their respective 'natural' environments. The regional authorities in each territory have been granted the right to sign agreements with neighbouring states for the purposes of economic, technical and cultural cooperation. To a large extent, however, these provisions remain a dead letter. The main impetus for this aspect of regional policy has not sprung spontaneously from some innate affinity of the Antilles or Reunion with their geographical neighbours, most of whom share a creole culture. Rather it comes from the geopolitical and cultural priorities of the French state, as this comment from Michel Rocard makes clear:

> Your future is right here in the Caribbean, and on the American continent. The more Guadeloupe and Martinique become part of the Caribbean, and the more French Guiana becomes part of South America, the better the interests and the voice of France will be defended and expressed (*Le Monde*, 8-9 April 1990).

CORSICA AND DECENTRALIZATION

Corsica is a Mediterranean island that belongs to both the French Republic and the European Union. It is a periphery that is geographically close but a periphery nevertheless. It could be described as a 'territorial minority' whose territory is a primary reference point in determining its identity. However, part of its population lives outside its natural territory and this constitutes a 'diaspora' within 'continental' France numbering between 400-500,000 individuals (the figures are difficult to ascertain). This has important consequences for an island whose population of around 220,000 occupies a territory of roughly 9,000 km².

Corsican history is marked by a long series of confrontations as some Corsicans continually opposed those states which attempted to integrate it. It has always been a periphery except for the period of the 'Corsican Revolution' (1729-1769) when, under Pascal Paoli, it achieved an ephemeral independence and the status of an independent Republic and finally became French in 1769. According to the Corsican historian Ettori (1982), the political and identity claims from this period have gone through four distinct phases:

1. The period between 1869 and 1896 was marked by a slow integration into the French polity; the cultural conflict between the French and Italian influences was definitively won by the former towards the second half of the 19th century under Napoleon III.
2. The period 1896-1940 saw the revival of cultural opposition with the appearance in 1896 of the first review in the Corsican language *A Tramuntana* (the name comes from a wind which blows over the whole island); this was followed in 1922 by a political revival in the form of an autonomist movement called the *Partitu Corsu d'Azione* (which became the *Partitu Corsu Autonomistu* in 1927); however, the fascist inclinations of these movements during the Mussolini period and during the occupation of Corsica (1940-1943) meant their demise in the post-war period.
3. The third period 1940-1965 was one of decline for the island: economic, demographic and cultural decline which the central government tried to stem with the *Plan d'Action Régional* of 1957. This plan was shelved when De Gaulle came to power in 1958 but was reactivated as a means of facilitating the reincorporation of around 17,000 *pied noir* settlers from Algeria following independence in 1962. Around 500 families settled as farmers on the *Plaine Orientale* and were given privileged treatment over the local Corsicans. While these events did bring about a certain kind of development (tourism and agriculture), their excesses provoked the final phase.
4. The final phase which is continuing until today is marked by the attempt of various movements to force the French government to recognise the specificity of the island rather than (in their eyes) its forced assimilation.

Regionalist Demands in the Post-War Period

It is necessary to analyze briefly the *mouvement revendicatif* which began in the early 1970s in order to grasp the constitutional evolution of the island [*Loughlin, 1989*]. Throughout this century, all Corsicans have been concerned with the economic and social decline of their island. However, particularly in the post-war period, as the crisis reached almost irreversible proportions, some Corsicans, such as the UPC *(Unione di U Populu Corsu)* and the FLNC *(Front de Libération Nationale de la Corse)* have been willing to advocate radical solutions (autonomy within France or complete independence) and to adopt extraparliamentary methods and even violence to achieve these. It is important to emphasize that most Corsicans remained loyal to France but the radical regionalists did sway public opinion into accepting many of their theses. In particular, almost all Corsicans were united in demanding greater control over their own affairs as a means of reversing the decline although they differed on the form this should take [*Loughlin, 1989*].

During the 1970s, there was a *rapprochement* between the Corsican regionalists and the socialist left (as occurred elsewhere in France). The new Socialist Party under Mitterrand and figures such as Michel Rocard, leader of the PSU *(Parti Socialiste Unifié)* began to modify their traditional jacobinism and to take on board in their programmes some of the regionalist theses. This harmonized well with the preoccupation with *autogéstion* characteristic of these years.

State Responses to the Corsican Problem

Right-wing governments under Pompidou and Giscard d'Estaing aggravated the situation in Corsica by adopting a heavy-handed approach to the island based largely on police repression although there were also half-hearted attempts to meet some of the regionalists' demands. Any constitutional recognition of Corsican specificity was totally excluded during this period. This changed with the election of François Mitterrand to President of the Republic and of the socialists in 1981. This was perceived as an opportunity for the Corsican regionalists to achieve some of their aims. Indeed, some of the demands of regionalists from different parts of France had been incorporated into the *110 Propositions du Candidat Mitterrand* before the election. During a public meeting in Ajaccio during the presidential election campaign in 1981, Mitterrand had announced that Corsica would receive a special statute. This promise became proposition 54 of the 110 propositions. In a communication to the regional council (*établissement public régional*) on 6 August 1981, Gaston Defferre, Minister of the Interior and

Decentralization summed up the government's plans as follows:

> Corsica has its own specificity, a cultural identity, a language, a culture, its own traditions and all this must be taken into account. When the government tackles the questions of decentralization and regionalization, it must approach the Corsican problem on its own terms ... The government proposes to you the creation of a new public authority (*collectivité territoriale de la République*) ... in conformity with Article 72 of the Constitution.

He also emphasized that the government wished to align the future statute of the island with that of Sicily and Sardinia in Italy. However, the final statute diverged considerably from this original intention.

The geographical and cultural specificity of Corsica would therefore be recognized and Corsicans would be given control over their economic development and the preservation and enrichment of their culture (Article 1 of the law of 2 March 1982 on the Special Statute of the Corsican Region). However, the expression '*peuple corse*' which was in the original version was removed from the final text. The French President explained why in a speech to the Corsican Assembly in June 1983: 'my government ... refused to separate the *peuple corse* from the *peuple français* and reaffirmed that Corsica forms part of the French Republic'. Furthermore, the distrust and even hostility of the right-wing opposition parties and the local elites (including the MRG *Mouvement des Radicaux de Gauche* - allegedly a pro-government party but in reality one of the two political clans of the island) forced the government to attenuate the most innovative parts of the law and to emphasize the preservation of national unity. This still did not prevent 94 deputies and 101 senators bringing the law to the Constitutional Council on 5 February 1982. However, the latter declared that the law generally was 'not in conflict with the Constitution' and went on to clarify the conditions of implementing the decentralization reforms.

With its new statute Corsica became a region, with institutions similar to those of the other French regions. It differed in that its elected body was called the Corsican Assembly (rather than simply a regional council) and it possessed two consultative committees. It also had more extensive powers in those fields relevant to the specific needs of the island: culture, transport, energy, planning, and education. In the end, the recognition of its specific character was confined within strict limits and even dissipated by the regionalization overseas and through the rest of France.

The most novel element was the unique capacity of the Corsican Assembly to communicate directly with the government (Article 27 of the law of 2 March 1982). Thus, the Assembly had the right to consult the government or be consulted by the government on all matters concerning Corsica. In this way, it had the right to remind the government of Corsica's special character when legislation was being prepared. However, these powers were very limited compared with those of the TOM (see above). Their powers of intervention are guaranteed by the Constitution and protected by the Constitutional Council which can use the fact of non-consultation as grounds for abrogating a law which affects the Territory. Furthermore, the Council ruled that the laws gave no legislative powers to the Corsican Region which has no power except that of soliciting the Prime Minister who is not obliged to follow their advice. The government showed itself willing to accept Corsican recommendations in domains related to technical and non-controversial issues: for example, the development and protection of the Corsican mountains (law 85-30 of 9 January 1985) or the protection and development of the coast (law 86-2 of 3 January 1986). However, when the matter was political or emanating from the regionalist groups it was met by refusal or indifference: propositions in favour of teaching the Corsican culture and language (July 1983); giving priority of Corsicans in local employment and the recognition of the 'Corsican people' (November 1983); creation of a special fiscal statute and a free exchange zone (April 1985), and so on. These proposals illustrated the limits of the capacity or willingness of the centre to respond to the demands of the Corsican periphery.

The laws of 10 July 1985 and 6 January 1986 further weakened the recognition of Corsica's special character. A circular from the Ministry of the Interior and Decentralization, dated 20 February 1986, made this explicit: 'all regions, including Ile-de-France, Corsica and those overseas, are from now on regulated by the law of 2 March 1982 and the modified law of 5 July 1972. These are the common legislative basis of the new regional institutions'. In effect, Corsica simply became another one of the 26 French regions. Added to this 'banalisation' of its statute, which was no longer very special, was a certain withdrawal by the state and the erratic functioning of the regional institutions in Corsica. This was a consequence of the institutional overload but also of the chronic instability of the Corsican Assembly. Over a period of ten years, there were no less than four elections to the Corsican Assembly. This situation led to the development of financial clientelism and discredited the regional government which came to be known as a 'super conseil général'. Political figures from all shades of the political spectrum were agreed that the government should introduce a new reform of its statute.

The New Statut Particulier

In contrast to 1981, there was no mention of reforms for Corsica during the presidential elections of 1988. Right to the end of 1989 different strategies were present even within the government. Nevertheless, on 29 September 1988, Pierre Joxe, Minister of the Interior, set up an interministerial committee, presided over by the Prime Minister, to deal with the cultural, economic and social development of Corsica. The committee aimed to formulate an approach to developing Corsica while respecting its special identity. After a meeting on 26 October 1989, the committee declared itself open to all propositions for reforming the special statute which might enhance the effectiveness of the regional institutions and give Corsicans greater control over their destiny. After wide consultations, Joxe announced his intentions on 23 May 1990 during a speech to local politicians. He drew up a list of reasons why the old statute had not functioned as it had been meant to and suggested a return to the original principles of the decentralization reforms. Of particular significance were his promises to incorporate a resolution of the Corsican Assembly on 13 October 1988 which called for the recognition of a *peuple corse* and his promises to give the Corsican institutions a legal basis different from that of the other (metropolitan) regions. On 31 October 1990, the Cabinet adopted a bill to create a statute for a *collectivité territoriale de Corse* to be placed before the National Assembly on 20 November. These developments created a political furore both in Corsica and in Parliament. However, the bill was passed on the third reading on 12 April 1991 by 276 votes to 262, with 38 abstentions and one absent. The bill was opposed by almost all opposition deputies, the MRG and those close to J. P. Chévènement's *'socialisme et république'* faction. The Senate, in its turn, opposed the bill and adopted a radically altered text. Finally, the Constitutional Council was engaged by the President of the Senate and more than half of the senators to examine the bill.

The new statute was original in a number of respects. It transformed a mainland region of France into a territorial authority *'sui generis'* placing the island in the same category as the 'peripheral territories'. It gave the island an institutional structure that was 'parastatal' which up to that point had been given only to the TOM. It entailed a reform of the electoral registers of the island's municipalities reducing the electoral body from 200,000 to 158,000 in order to counter the evils of electoral fraud. It revamped the mechanism of consultation with the central government to bring this more into line with that of the DOM/TOM.

However, the issue which sparked off ferocious opposition was Article 1 of the new law. Several aspects of this article merit attention. First, it refers explicitly to the *'peuple corse'* defined as a 'living cultural and historical community'. This largely followed the resolution of the Corsican Assembly of 13 October 1988 declaring the existence of a 'Corsican people'. This gave a political character to the new statute which made it more than a simple decentralization law. Several other aspects of the article merit attention. It also refers to *'le peuple corse, composante du peuple français'*. Although this was condemned by the Corsican nationalists as demeaning, some of them later regretted that it was dropped since it allowed one to think of the 'French people' as a plural entity made up of different elements without questioning the indivisibility and sovereignty of the nation. As D. Rousseau emphasized: 'The Joxe proposal ... by describing the Corsican people as a part of the whole *(composante)*, attempted to modernize the term "section" [of the French people] ... [while] the statute would in no way affect national sovereignty' *(Libération*, 21 November 1990). According to this analysis the constitutional principle of indivisibility did not apply to the 'people' but to the exercise of the 'sovereignty of the people'. Another noteworthy feature of Article 1 is that it stipulated that the French Republic guaranteed to uphold for this community those rights that were connected to its geographical insularity. The article filled in the detail of these *droits liés à l'insularité* by mentioning 'the preservation of cultural identity and the defence of specific economic and social interests'. It thereby underlined the two fields to which public authorities should give priority attention – cultural and economic development – while insisting that the Republic would 'guarantee' this development.

The recognition of Corsica's special character was thus based on its geographical features. This was to preempt any attempts by other French regions to claim similar prerogatives for their regions. At the same time, it left open the possibility for other insular regions such as the DOM to reform their institutional structures. The implication was that insularity could be the basis of granting statutes with a great deal of autonomy different from those which emanated from simple administrative decentralization.

By striking down Article 1 of the new statute, the French Constitutional Council annulled, at a stroke, the political foundations of the government's initiative. However, the other elements of the statute do remain.

The Influence of the European Union on Corsica's Constitutional Development

The importance of European integration for Corsica is a recent phenomenon. It must be remembered that, until 1983, the European Commission had placed Corsica in the Provence-Alpes-Côtes d'Azur (PACA). The first battle related to the EU concerned the separation of Corsica from PACA. The subsequent Community enlargements of the 1980s and the development of

EC regional policy were also important for the island's position in Europe. Thus, instead of the confrontation between Corsica and the French Republic there developed a three-sided relationship in which the Community would play an increasingly important role thanks to its growing regional policy. This would have an impact on the development of the new statute of 1992.

During the parliamentary debates on the special statute one of the arguments put forward by Joxe to justify the reforms of the statute was that Corsica should benefit from a statute aligned with those of Europe's other island communities. In an interview with *Le Monde* he declared that 'in a democratic Europe all island regions should have special statutes' (28 June 1990). During a conference at Ajaccio on this theme which Joxe organized, it was shown that most islands within the EC had special statutes which took into account their special circumstances and which involved numerous derogations from the common law of their countries. A report of a parliamentary commission on constitutional law also pointed out the position of the Spanish, Portuguese, Italian and British islands. Finally, a report prepared for the Senate compared the statutes drawn up by Denmark for the Faroes and Greenland, Spain for the Balearics and the Canaries, Portugal for the Azores and Madeira, Italy for Sicily and Sardinia and the UK for the Isle of Man. It was pointed out that, among the large islands of the Community, only Crete did not have a special statute.

However, the government's arguments based on the existence of these various statutes were based more on symbolism than on any real desire to tackle the constitutional issues involved. In reality, to achieve a greater degree of internal autonomy in France would have meant a constitutional revision of the French state which was not on the cards.

The Functioning of the New Corsican Statue

Since the regional elections in Corsica in March 1992, it has not been possible to draw up a provisional assessment of the functioning of the new statute. However, some comments by way of conclusion would be in order. First, those who were in favour of the reform of the Corsican statute did not emerge as winners following the extensive debate which occurred during the preparation of the statute. On the contrary, the coalition which took power in the Corsican Assembly included the MRG, who were profoundly hostile to the reform. The MRG managed to gain two places out of seven on the executive, with the other seats going to parties of the national opposition also hostile to the reform. Second, the elections showed a continuing fragmentation of the Corsican political class. During the first round there were 13 lists: two nationalist lists; five from the left including two socialist and two communist; and six from the right with divisions in the UDF and

RPR groups. This fragmentation was a consequence both of the electoral system of PR and of the divisions within all the political groups (except the MRG) between those accepting and those opposing the new statute. Finally, the concurrent cantonal elections did not help to reinforce the 'regional' character of the elections. However, what was noteworthy about these elections was that while the national opposition parties as a whole received 51 per cent of the votes, the Corsican nationalist parties received 25 per cent (an increase of 12 percentage points compared with the regional elections of 1986). The great losers were the left with the disappearance of the socialists, the collapse of the MRG and decline of the communists.

The period since these elections has been marked by the slowness with which the new institutions have been set up. Finally, it could be concluded that the new institutions and the new special statute will do little to remedy the chronic political backwardness and instability of the island.

CONCLUSION

In the past, within a Jacobin administrative and ideological framework, it was taken for granted that regions with a marked cultural distinctiveness were French first and foremost. This applied to Corsica and Brittany as well as to Reunion and Martinique. The construction of a 'new Europe' in the post-Cold War period implies, however, some hardening of notions of difference between Europe and the rest of the world; the creation of a common west European identity may jeopardize the idea of French citizenship, which is based on a legal and juridical rather than a kith and kin-based national identity.

Yet the ties that bind maritime France, and the overseas departments in particular, to continental France, are strong and resilient: they include the movement back and forth of people between the mainland, the Antilles, French Guiana and Reunion. Almost half of all Antilleans and one third of Reunionnese now live, or were born, in continental France. The danger is that with recession and the rise of far-right politics in France, these 'negropolitans' may develop a growing sense of cultural and economic exclusion, which could feed back into local regional politics in the DOM. One response may be a marked radicalization of the tone of the political debate: the hostility to the 'big bad wolf' of the Common Market was one expression of this. An increase in pro-independence sentiments may be another.

This introductory presentation of the French overseas territories has attempted to show that it is an illusion to see them as one uniform category (see Table 7:2). The 'ten little Frances', the 'confetti', which are all that remains of France's past colonial *grandeur*, are united by a set of problems

TABLE 7:2
GEOGRAPHICAL AND POLITICAL INDICATORS ON OVERSEAS FRANCE

Territory	Population	Surface area Km²	Density inh/Km²	Constitutional Status	Parliam. Rep. Nat. Ass.	Parliam. Rep. Senate	Territorial Rep. Council	Territorial Rep. Exec.	Geopolitical Region
Territory	Population	rea Km2	inh/Km22	Constitutional					Geopolitical
Guadeloupe	400.000	1,780	224	Commun:lois 13/ 4 déc. '82, org. régions d'Outre-Mer; 2/08/'84 "Compétences"	2	41	41	Caribbean	Caribbean
Martinique	368.000	1,106	332		4	2	31		L. America L.
Guyanne	114.000	90,000	1		2	1	45		Indian Ocean
Réunion	620.000	2,512	246		5	3			
(above = DOM) (art. 73c of Const.)	1,502,600 (16,36%)	95,398 (18.35%)	15		15	8	158	Exec. des régions	
Nelle Calédonie	170.000	19,103	9	L. Réf. 8/11/88	2	1	54	Haut-C.	South Pacific
Polynésie Franç-	180.000	4,200	42	L. 06/09/84	2	1	41	Gouv. Ter.	"
Wallis et Futuna	12,500	280	44	L. 19/07/61	1	1	25	Adm. Terr.	"
(above = TOM) (art. 74c of Const.)	362,500 (16,36%)	23,583 (18.35%)	16	Varie en fonction des spécificités des TOM	5	3	120	Variable	
St. Pierre et Miqueulon	6,892	242	26	L. 11/06/85	1	1	19	Prés/V.Pr.	N. America
Mayotte	94,410	374	252	L. 24/12/76	1	1	17	Préfet	Canal Moz
Corsica	249,000	8,872	28	L. 13/05/91	4	2	51	Cons. Exé.	Mediterranean
(above = Collectiv. Territoriales) (art. 72c of Const.)	349,802 (15,79%)	9,488 (7,88%)	37	Variable	6	4	87	Variable	
TOTAL Outre Mer	2,214,902 (100%)	128,469 (100%)	17		26	15	367		
TOTAL FRANCE	57,2 Mil.	547,026	104		577	321			

Source: État du Monde 1994; Annuaire économique et géopolitique mondial.
ED.: La Decouverte, sept. 1993.

resulting from their insularity. Jean-François Auby has suggested the term 'collectivités périphériques françaises' to describe these territories. They remain territories which are defined as 'part of the Nation, but with historical, geographical, economic and political characteristics that require them to be granted an exceptional status, distinct from that of other components of the Republic' [*Auby, 1992: 10*]. However, such efforts at classification should not lead us to forget that law is a product of social relations, and that under the 'legal garments' are human communities who live, hope and create projects for a better future.

Perhaps one of the most significant developments has been the slow and rather grudging recognition by the French state of this diversity. Furthermore, Corsica has also been included within these 'special' peripheral regions. What we are witnessing is a series of constitutional experiments, carried out often as a result of pressure from the peripheries, which are modifying the old uniform constitutional structure of the French Republic. The different territorial entities – DOM, TOM and Corsica – are learning from each other although Corsica and the TOM seem to be in the forefront of constitutional innovation. However, constitutional innovation, although essential in a state such as France where public policy is to a large extent constrained by public law and constitutional features, is a necessary but not sufficient condition to bring about the political, social and economic development of the territories involved. As can be seen from the Corsican case, new regional institutions have not solved the chronic problems of political instability and economic and social underdevelopment. There is still a need for considerable intervention by the central state and, increasingly, the European Union.

NOTES

1. Comité National chargé de la publication des travaux préparatoires des Institutions de la Vème République; Doucement pour servir à l'Histoire de l'élaboration de la Constition du 4 octobre 1958, Volume no. 1, p. 106; la Documentation française, 1er trim. 1987. This position would also appear in the constitutional law of 3 June 1958: 'La Consitution doit permettre d'organiser les rapports de la République avec les peuples qui lui sont associés'.

REFERENCES

Albrechts, L. *et al.*, 1989, *Regional Policy at the Crossroads: European Perspectives* (London: Jessica Kingsley/Regional Studies Association).

Auby, J. F., 1992, *Les Statuts des Territoires d'outre-mer* (Paris: PUF, Coll. Droit Fondamental).

Castor, E., and G. Othily, 1984, *La Guyane: Les Grands Problèmes les Solutions Possibles* (Paris: Editions Caribéennes).

Catteau, C. *et al.*, 1992, 'Le RMI à la Réunion; une famille sur quatre en bénéficie', *Economie et Statistique*, 252, March, pp.51-62.

Chagnollaud, D., 1991, 'Les DOM-TOM', *Bilan Politique de la France 1991* (Paris: Hachette), pp.71-75.

Chane-Kune, S., 1991, 'Le Chaudron Reunionnais', *Herodote*, 62, pp.91-100.

CGP - Commissariat General du Plan, 1983, *Préparation du IXème Plan 1984-88*, Tome 5,6, (Paris: La Documentation Française).

Constant, F., 1988, *La Retraite aux Flambeaux Société et Politique en Martinique* (Paris: Editions Caribéennes).

DAN - *Débats de l'Assemblée Nationale*, 1981, Michel Debré, 10 January 1981, pp.326-7 (Paris: La Documentation Française).

De Baleine, P., 1980, *Les Danseuses de la France* (Paris: Plon).

De Gaulle, C., 1980, *Memoires de Guerre: Tome III. Le Salut 1944–1946* (Paris: Presse Pocket).

Ettori, F., 1981, 'Langue et Littérature', in ouvrage collectif, *Corse* (Paris: Bonneton).

Le Monde, Dossiers et Documents, 1992, 'Dix ans de decentralisation', September.

Fortune, F-H., 1989, 'L'évolution du discours gaulliste vis-à-vis des DOM', *Antilla*, 345, 7-13 August.

Gore, C., 1984, *Regions in Question, Space, Development Theory and Regional Policy* (London and New York: Methuen).

Gilroy, P., 1992, 'The End of Racism', in J. Donal (ed.), *'Race', Culture and Difference* (London: Sage/Open University), pp.49-61.

Guillebaud, C., 1979, *Les Confettis de l'Empire*.

Hall, S., 1992, 'Our Mongrel Selves', *New Society*, With Channel 4 Borderlands, 4 May.

Hintjens, H., 1991, 'Regional Reform in the French Periphery: The Overseas Departments of Reunion, Martinique and Guadeloupe', *Regional Politics and Policy*, 1(1), pp.51-73.

Jolivet, M-J., 1990, 'Entre autochtones et immigrants: diversité et logique des positions créoles guyanaises', *Etudes Créoles*, XIII, (2), pp.11-32.

Lacoste, Y., 1991, 'Les Territoires de la Nation', *Herodote*, 62, pp.3-21.

Loughlin, J., 1989, *Regional and Ethnic Nationalism in France: A Case-study of Corsica* (Florence: European University Institute).

MacDonald, S., and A. Gastmann, 1984, 'Mitterand's Headache: The French Antilles in the 1980s', *Caribbean Review*, 13.

McDougall, D., 1986, *The Mitterand Presidency and France's Overseas Possessions, 1981-86*, unpublished paper Department of International Relations, Australia National University, 12 June.

Mathieu, J-L., 1988, *Les DOM-TOM* (Paris: Presses Universitaires Françaises).

Reno, F., 1993, *Les Départements Français de la Caraïbe et l'Europe Communautaire: les nouvelles données de la dépendance*, paper presented to the 17th Annual Conference Society for Caribbean Studies, Oxford: 6-8 July.

Ziller, J. 1991, *Les Dom-Tom: Collection 'Systêmes'* (Paris: LGDJ, Cahors France).

French Regions and the European Union

SONIA MAZEY

INTRODUCTION[1]

1992 witnessed the completion of the Single European Market (SEM). It also marked the 10th anniversary of the ambitious French decentralization reforms introduced by the first Mitterrand government in 1982. Initiated in response to different problems and concerns, these two developments have subsequently become bound up with each other. Though not officially recognized as partners in the founding treaties of the EC, regional and local authorities throughout the Union have, since the early 1980s, become more involved in the EU policy process. This development has occurred largely as a result of two simultaneous trends in European politics – regionalization and European integration. Since the 1970s, subnational governments throughout the EU (with the notable exception of the United Kingdom) have acquired important new responsibilities and legislative powers [*Sharpe, 1979* and *1993*]. In France, the 1982 *Defferre* reforms accorded the newly-created regional governments significant policy responsibilities in the fields of infrastructure planning and socio-economic development. In carrying out this role, French regions (like their European counterparts) have increasingly had to operate within a European rather than a national context. This development has created new opportunities and constraints for regions. Initially attracted to Brussels by the prospect of EU funding for regional development programmes, regional representatives have latterly been forced to consider the regional impact of the SEM and EU legislation. In this context, the ratification of the 1986 Single European Act and the establishment of the 1 January 1993 deadline for the completion of the Single European Market marked important turning points. Successive French governments since 1986 have become increasingly convinced of the need to adapt French regional administrative structures to the European market environment in order to ensure effective coordination of EU policy.

Meanwhile, the European Commission, anxious to minimize regional disparities within the SEM has, since the mid-1980s, sought to develop a more coherent EU regional policy, based upon the principle of 'partnership' with regional and local authorities. Growing commitment to the now fashionable principle of 'subsidiarity' has further persuaded EU officials and MEPs of the need to incorporate regional interests more fully into the EU policy process. The regional dimension of EU policy-making has thus acquired a new salience. This commitment is reflected in the doubling of the Community's structural funds between 1989 and 1993, EU Commission support for interregional economic cooperation and provision in the Maastricht Treaty for the formal representation of regional interests at the EU level in a new Committee of the Regions. The 'Europeanization' of regional government is not merely a national phenomenon; the past few years have also witnessed a proliferation of EU-wide regional associations and cross-frontier regional policy networks whose members have a common interest in particular EU policy outcomes. These developments have resulted in new patterns of intergovernmental relations within the Union and given fresh impetus to regionalist hopes of a 'Europe of the Regions'.

The wider political consequences of these developments are, however, contradictory. On the one hand, European integration *has* provided regional governments and regional associations with new opportunities for economic intervention, increased policy influence and political status. At the same time, however, the primacy of EU law (and the need to ensure its effective application) throughout the Community has imposed new legal limits to regional autonomy. EU policy-making procedures (for example, with respect to the allocation of EU structural funds) also continue to underline the power of central governments. European integration is thus in some respects a centralizing process [*Biancarelli, 1991*].

This paper examines the developments outlined above in the case of France (though similar trends are apparent throughout the EU). It is argued that the *Defferre* reforms were important in facilitating the 'Europeanization' of French regional policy-making. By extending the economic powers and political legitimacy of the French regional authorities, these reforms provided both the incentive and the necessary institutional framework for the articulation of regional interests at the EU level. Regional political and socio-economic elites, not surprisingly, were initially attracted to Brussels by the prospect of additional funds. The continuing importance of this consideration is reflected in the considerable weight of the French regional lobby in Brussels. Anticipation of the regional impact of the SEM also proved an influential catalyst for interregional cooperation; the 1982 regional reforms provided the financial and legal basis for the establishment of such links. However, regional political autonomy with regard to EU matters remains limited. Whilst successive French governments have generally backed the regions in their quest for EU funding they have repeatedly stressed the functional *raison d'être* of the regions (that is, in terms of national economic development and planning) and insisted upon the constitutional supremacy of the state with regard to EU decision-making and external affairs. Indeed, as Delcamp [*1993*] points out, the growing importance of EU policies (notably regional policy) for the regions after

1986, persuaded French national governments of the need to reinforce the state administrative structures at the regional level. This concern is reflected in the 1992 territorial administrative reform which strengthened the authority of the regional prefect. Thus, in the French case, European integration has prompted two interrelated developments at the regional level. On the one hand, the prospect of interregional competition within the SEM has convinced governments of the need for administrative *déconcentration*. Meanwhile, regional (and local) elected authorities are themselves becoming more directly involved in the EU policy process. In consequence, the situation is now one of 'perforated sovereignty' [*Duchacek, 1990*] where international relations (at least with regard to 'low politics' issues) is a significant concern for sub-national as well as national governments. European integration has also prompted the emergence of new regional groupings and processes which transcend the territorial and legal parameters of 'old' regions defined by the nation-state. The present situation is thus one of flux: whilst the state remains the key EU interlocutor and an important EU lobbyist for French regional interests, there are signs that regional authorities are themselves becoming more influential with regard to the EU policy process. The wider political and constitutional significance of these developments is as yet unclear. However, it would appear that bilateral models of EU policy-making which focus solely upon the relationship between the EU and member-states have been rendered obsolete.

The following discussion is divided into three parts. Part one outlines briefly the principal features of the 1982 regional reforms and explains their importance in providing an institutional core around which regional socio-economic interests have been able to coalesce. Part two highlights the growing relevance of European Union legislation for French regional authorities since the mid-1980s. Part three examines in more detail the representation of French regional interests in the EU policy process, the French regional lobby in Brussels and the participation of French regional governments and groups in transnational regional networks. The paper concludes with an evaluation of these developments and considers the wider implications of them for centre-periphery relations both within France and the EU.

THE 1982 *DEFFERRE* REFORMS: CONSOLIDATING FRENCH REGIONAL NETWORKS AND INSTITUTIONAL CORES

The 1982 decentralization programme introduced by the newly-elected socialist government of François Mitterrand was not prompted by reflections on the future role of France within the European Union, but by *national* socio-economic and political concerns. More specifically, decentralization was a response to the widespread feeling that the French state had become impotent yet omnipresent [*Delcamp, 1993: 58*]. The declared objective of these reforms was to devolve powers and responsibilities from Paris to directly elected local and regional governments. In short, the French state was to be decentralized and democratized in accordance with the socialists' long-standing electoral promise. However, France was to remain a unitary state and there was no intention to transform it into a federation. Moreover, whilst the socialists were anxious to reform the state, they never intended to weaken it. As the then Prime Minister, Pierre Mauroy explained 'the more one decentralizes, the more necessary is it for there to be a strong state presence' (*Débats Assemblée nationale*, 8 July 1981). Thus, political decentralization was to be balanced by administrative deconcentration.[2] In the context of this discussion, the key point is that despite the shortcomings of these reforms, they provided a regional politico-administrative framework which later formed the basis for the incorporation of French regional interests into the EU policy-making process. Essentially, the 1982 *Defferre* reforms completed the piecemeal development of regional government in France in the Fifth Republic [*Dayries and Dayries, 1986*].

The effect of these changes was to create regional politico-administrative structures, identifiable regional interests and regional political elites. By the mid-1980s there existed at the regional level a network of interests (represented by politicians and officials, public agencies, credit institutions, chambers of commerce and small- and medium-sized enterprises [SMEs] which could be mobilized by reference to a *regional* identity. Significantly, Article 65 of the *Defferre* law of 2 March 1982 empowered French regions to enter into cross-frontier cooperation agreements with local authorities in neighbouring countries within the juridical framework of an 'association' (subject to national government authorization) [*Dolez, 1992: 39*]. This was a crucial facilitating factor in the subsequent development of European regional cooperation. The functional responsibilities and powers accorded to French regions by the 1982 regional reforms further paved the way for a closer relationship between the elected regional authorities and the European Union.

The reforms also granted regions a primary role in the formulation and implementation of the national economic plan [*Mazey, 1987 and 1993*] Regional chairpersons have, since 1982, been *de facto* members of the national planning commission where the general priorities of the national plan are determined. In addition, regional development plans drawn up by the regional prefect in collaboration with the regional council have, since 1982, formed the basis for a series of planning contracts (*contrats de plan*) signed by the regional authority and the state. Each contract commits the region and the state (and typically local authorities, private and public sector bodies) to the joint financing of a series of development projects for the duration of the national plan. These procedures were used for the Xth Plan (1989-1992) and, in a revised form, for the XIth Plan (1993-96). In practice, regionalization of the planning process has been relatively limited; consultation with interested parties has in many cases been minimal and national planning priorities have tended to prevail over regional ones, especially with regard to the allocation of state finance [*Rémond and Blanc, 1989: 359-76*]. Nevertheless, at the very least, these procedures prompted regional authorities to consider the region's strategic location within the SEM. Indeed, they were encouraged to do so by the government. The central objective of the Xth Plan (1989-1992) according to Lionel Stoléru, Secretary of State in charge of the Plan, was to prepare France for the opening of the SEM [*Deslhiat, 1989: 9*]. Regional authorities were urged by the national planning authorities to give priority to the economic impact of the SEM in formulating their regional plans. Moreover, as Gaston Defferre, Minister for Planning made clear, the government's primary objective in the Xth Plan was to bring about a convergence between national investment strategies on the one hand and EU regional funding priorities as reflected in 'Community Interest Programmes' (CIPs) on the other. (*Le Monde*, 16 January 1986). To this end, since 1990, the French planning agency DATAR has provided training sessions for local administrators on EU structural funds [*Plainfosse, 1993*]. The regional and contractual characteristics of the French planning process as developed in the 1980s provided a suitable administrative mechanism for realizing this objective. Since 1984, several French regions, supported by the central government, have successfully negotiated trilateral planning contracts between the region, the state and the EU. As part of the Integrated Mediterranean Programme, for instance, five French regions (Aquitaine, Corsica, Languedoc-Roussillon, Midi-Pyrénées, Provence-Alpes-Côte-d'Azur) and two *départements* (Drôme and Ardèche) received a total of FF9 billion from the EU between 1986 and 1989 to help finance 7,000 infrastructure projects agreed between the Commission and the regional authorities (*Libération*, 18 July 1987). One purpose of French regional lobbyists in Brussels is to try to ensure that EU structural fund allocation rules are favourable to French regional investment strategies.

THE REGIONAL IMPACT OF EUROPEAN INTEGRATION

Little attention was paid to the impact of European integration upon local and regional governments before the adoption of the single market programme in 1985. Hull and Rhodes [*1977*] concluded from a study of the impact of EU legislation on local government in Britain and West Germany that the Community had 'a direct but *limited* impact on sub-national authorities'. The 1992 programme for the completion of the single European market fundamentally changed this situation. As Bongers observed in the case of the UK:

> The 1992 process is not aimed particularly at local government, but its impact will be profound in many fields affecting local authorities' responsibilities ... The completion of the single European market will bring major changes in the way in which the UK is governed. These changes will affect every sector of society, they will affect every service provided by local government and, potentially at least, they will affect the constitutional position of local government in its relationship to the state [*Bongers, 1990*].

The 1992 programme which seeks to remove physical, technical and fiscal barriers to the free movement of goods, services, capital and labour within the Union covers a number of policy sectors which typically fall within local and/or regional authority competence. These include regional economic development and planning (and the attraction of external investment), vocational and professional training, local transport (both public and private), the supply and maintenance of public utilities, housing provision for EU migrants, environmental policies, trading standards, health and safety in the workplace, and consumer protection law [*Raux, 1991*]. It is impossible to examine all these areas in detail; the following examples are merely illustrative.

The Legislative Impact of the 1992 Programme

A key area of EU legislation of direct concern to regional and local authorities includes rules governing regional aid provided either by the state and/or regional authorities (Article 92 of the Treaty of Rome). Attempts by the European Commission since the mid-1980s to establish a more effective EU-wide regional policy have served to reduce the degree of autonomy enjoyed by national and regional authorities in this area [*Auby, 1990*]. In December 1990, for instance, the French government was forced by the European Commission to withdraw development grants from 20 departments which did not meet EU guidelines for regional assistance. The European Commission also threatened to take legal action against the French over industrial restructuring grants awarded by the latter to six public companies including Electricité de France, Elf-Aquitaine, Thomson, Péchiney, EMC and Rhône-Poulenc (*Le Figaro,* 21 December 1990; *Le Monde,* 25 December 1990). This single example highlights the degree to which French economic planners (including regional authorities) are now constrained by EU regulations. Awareness of this fact has prompted concerted EU lobbying on the part of the French Planning Minister and regional administrations anxious to ensure that EU regulations governing regional aid are favourable to their interests (*Le Monde*, 10 March 1989: 18 July 1989).

EU Public Procurement Directives which came into force in 1989 and 1990 have far-reaching implications for regional and local authorities. All public supply and maintenance contracts – including those in the previously excluded sectors of energy, water, transport and telecommunications – valued at 130,000 ECU and all public works contracts in these sectors worth five million ECU or more must conform to EU rules. Contracts must be advertised in the Official Journal of the EU and must not discriminate against non-national firms (for example, by specifying national rather than EU technical standards). This legislation is of direct concern to French local and regional authorities, which in 1988 were responsible for 75 per cent of total public investment in France and for 20 per cent of all public contracts, a figure which rises to 40 per cent in the field of building/civil engineering[3] [*Delcamp, 1992: 50*].

Single market legislation aimed at establishing the free movement of labour within the Union also directly affects local and regional authorities both as major public employers and as providers of housing, welfare and education for EU migrants. As employers, French regional authorities are bound to comply with Union social policy and legislation based upon the EU Social Charter. More specifically, regional authorities must comply with EU legislation relating to health and safety at work, work-related benefits and worker representation. The European Commission has also sought since the mid-1980s to restrict the number of public administration posts which, under Article 48 of the Treaty of Rome, may be reserved for nationals. In a Communication dated 18 March 1988, the Commission stated that only those regional authority positions involving the legal representation of the state may be reserved for French nationals. All other administrative positions, including local authority posts must be open to EU nationals.

In reality, the SEA and the 1992 programme have multiple legal implications for French regional authorities, which must now apply EU technical and safety standards, for example, with respect to sewage levels in sea water and health and safety standards in the workplace. In the educational field, regional authorities are responsible for the provision of vocational and language training (to facilitate the free movement of labour). Regional governments are also responsible for carrying out EU environmental impact assessments in connection with major industrial and infrastructure projects. Other aspects of the single market programme have important *indirect* consequences for regional authorities. For example, the introduction of a common transport policy (deemed to be necessary for the effective functioning of the single market) will require the harmonization of local speed limits and public transport subsidies. Recent moves to harmonize indirect taxation levels throughout the Union have prompted concern among French regional politicians, since the levels of state funding for French regional and local authorities are linked to the level of VAT revenue received by the state.

The Economic Impact of the 1992 Programme

In addition to the legislative impact of the 1992 programme upon regional authorities, the latter must also respond to the socio-economic impact of the SEM. The Cecchini report prepared for the European Commission, predicted that completion of the internal market would create 1.8 million additional jobs, lead to a six per cent fall in consumer prices and boost economic growth rates within the Union [*Cecchini, 1988*]. However, the predicted benefits of the internal market, even if realized, will not be evenly distributed throughout the EU. Certain industrial sectors and less favoured regions are likely to be adversely affected by the increased competition resulting from the removal of trade barriers. Geographically, the 1992 programme favours the core regions of the Union and discriminates against the periphery. The so-called 'Golden Triangle' (or 'Golden Banana') covering the areas between Birmingham, Milan, Paris and the Ruhr constitutes the prosperous core of the EU. Areas of northern Italy westward to southern France and eastern Spain are also experiencing rapid economic growth. The periphery includes the northern regions of the UK, Corsica, southern Italy, Greece, Portugal and Ireland. In sectoral terms, vulnerable sectors include those which have high non-tariff barriers, but low levels of intra-EU trade – for example, mining, steel, shipbuilding [*Gallacher, 1989; Labasse 1991*].

Within the EU, France is regarded as a relatively wealthy region. Nevertheless, within France there are significant regional economic disparities. The capital region of Ile-de-France together with the eastern frontier regions of Alsace and Rhône-Alpes constitute the wealthier core. The periphery (economically speaking) includes regions such as Brittany, Nord-Pas-de-Calais (also suffering from industrial decline), Corsica and the overseas regions. Central and south-western rural regions such as Limousin and the Midi-Pyrénées are also relatively disadvantaged in socio-economic terms [*Labasse, 1991*]. A BVA poll carried out in 1990 of 2,111 heads of the top 10,000 French companies confirmed that the French regions most favoured by business for location purposes were Ile-de-France, Rhône-

Alpes and Alsace. These regions were believed to be the most dynamic and to offer the best political and economic benefits to firms. Least preferred were the regions of the Centre, Basse-Normandie, Poitou-Charente and Limousin (*Le Quotidien de Paris*, 13 February 1990). The same poll revealed that in view of the imminent opening of the SEM, 46 per cent of company directors believed regional authorities should give priority to establishing links with companies in other member-states; 25 per cent thought the regional councils should defend regional economic interests at the EU level, and 24 per cent relied upon the regional authority for information on EU legislation. [*Perrin, 1990: 47*]. Economic competitiveness within the SEM has thus become a major concern for French socio-economic elites, who believe that the regional authorities should support them in Brussels. It is important to bear in mind, however, that for many socio-economic interests (especially large companies), sectoral and trade associations along with links with national politico-administrative elites remain the principal conduits for national and EU lobbying.

At the national level, there has been considerable political debate since 1958 over the optimum size and number of French regions required for administrative and planning purposes. This debate was given fresh impetus by the statement by Jacques Delors, president of the EU Commission in 1988 that:

> ... 1992 Europe will need powerful regions; it will rely on zones of economic synergy where the departmental level is too small ... Today, France is handicapped compared to federal Germany or Spain (*Libération*, 2 October 1988).

Since 1988, French national governments have been concerned to ensure that French regions are able to compete effectively within the SEM. Thus, in February 1992, territorial administrative reforms were introduced which strengthened the coordinating powers of the regional prefect and established the hierarchical power of the regional prefect over his departmental counterpart. Proposals to reduce the number of regions to between 10 and 13 in order to make them more competitive with the German Länder have predictably been opposed by regional *notables* (*Le Monde*, 9 April 1989; *Le Quotidien de Paris*, 4 February 1989). Convinced of the need to strengthen French regions within the SEM, the government and the French planning agency DATAR have given their support to the regional federations of the *Grand Sud* and the *Grand Est*, established by regional politicians in the 1980s. They have also stressed the need for voluntary cooperation between French municipalities, local and regional authorities in the fields of research, transport and infrastructure programmes. A government proposal presented by Pierre Joxe, Minister of the Interior, to the National Association of Regional Politicians (ANER) in February 1990 proposed the creation of regional federations comprising two or more regions. As voluntary associations these would cooperate in policy sectors such as training, transport, research and university education. As an incentive, Joxe proposed that regions which cooperated in such schemes be given more powers than those which refused to [*Perrin, 1990; La Croix*, 25 June 1990]. This proposal was greeted with little enthusiasm by regional politicians, who have jealously guarded their autonomy with respect to interregional cooperation (*La Croix*, 25 February 1990). In a similar vein, Jacques Chérèque, Minister for Planning, warned that France was losing out to 'those torchlight cities near our borders' in the competition for foreign investment and stressed the need for 'solidarity between different territories by linking the medium-sized towns with each other so as to create metropolitan areas of European dimensions' (*La Tribune de l'Economie*, 25 May 1990).

The French government's support for regional federations is in large part a response to the growing importance since 1986 of EU regional policy and the associated structural funds. EU regional policy dates from the establishment of the European Regional Development Fund (ERDF) in 1975. Between 1975 and 1986 the size of the ERDF increased from 258 million ECU (4.8 per cent of the EU budget) to 3.1 billion ECU (8.6 per cent of the EU budget) [*Doutriaux, 1991: 21*]. Until 1984, 95 per cent of the ERDF was simply allocated to EU member-states in accordance with a national quota system and used to support nationally determined regional policies. The replacement of rigid quotas by 'indicative allocations' and the introduction of Programme Assistance in 1984, designed to increase the Commission's influence over the allocation of ERDF assistance, had little impact in practice. The ERDF remained 'a regional fund operated on a Red Cross basis with handouts here and there' (John Hume, MEP, quoted in *Shackleton, 1990*).

Following the adoption of the single market programme by the EU Heads of State in 1985, the Commission proposed a major overhaul of EU regional policy in an attempt to strengthen 'cohesion' within the SEM. The 1986 Single European Act set out the general principles of the proposed changes (Articles 130A and 130C) which were subsequently endorsed at the European Council in February 1988. At this meeting the EU Heads of State agreed to a doubling in real terms of the size of the structural funds from their 1987 level of 7,000 million ECU (19 per cent of the EU budget) to 14 million ECU (25 per cent of the EU budget) by 1993 [*Commission of the EC, 1990: 7*].[4] In accordance with new procedures, these funds were allocated to multi-annual (1989-93) programmes known as Community

Support Frameworks (CSFs), deemed by the EU Commission to be compatible with the five funding Objectives agreed by EU member-states (see Table 8.1). The shift away from annual project-by-project funding to multiannual financing of programmes fitted well with the five-year phases of the French Plan. In addition to the CSFs, the Commission allocated a further 3.8 billion ECU to EU Initiatives of Community Interest (CIPs). These initiatives (see Table 8.2) are primarily designed to promote regional development by creating the conditions in which indigenous enterprise can flourish [*Bohan, 1992*].

EU structural fund reforms also specified two new guiding principles of EU regional policy, partnership and additionality. The principle of partnership reflects the Commission's commitment to involving people and organizations at all levels – local, regional, national and EU – at each stage in the Fund's operation. The additionality principle means that EU funds should be used in conjunction with (not instead of) national and regional assistance. ERDF support, for instance, reimburses 50 per cent of the costs incurred by regional or local authorities and the state, providing the latter

TABLE 8.1
COMMUNITY SUPPORT FRAMEWORKS FINANCING BY OBJECTIVE AND
MEMBER-COUNTRY

COUNTRY	OBJECTIVE 1	OBJECTIVE 2	OBJECTIVES 3 AND 4	OBJECTIVE 5
BELGIUM	–	195.0	174.0	32.5
DENMARK	–	30.0	99.0	23.0
GERMANY	–	355.0	573.0	525.0
GREECE	–	6,667.0	–	–
SPAI N	9,779.0	735.0	563.0	285.0
FRANCE	888.0	700.0	872.0	960.0
IRELAND	3,672.0	–	–	–
ITALY	7,443.0	265.0	585.0	385.0
LUXEMBOURG	–	95.0	7.0	2.5
NETHERLANDS	–	15.0	230.0	44.0
PORTUGAL	6,958.0	–	–	–
U.K.	793.0	1,150.0	1,025.0	350.0
EC 12	36,200.0	3,900.0	4,128.0	2,607.0

Explanatory Note: Structural fund assistance is targeted on five priorities: lagging regions, that is, where GNP per head is no more than 75 per cent of EC average (Objective 1); declining industrial regions (Objective 2); assistance for the long-term unemployed (Objective 3) and integration of young people into the labour force (Objective 4); adjustment of agricultural structures (Objective 5a) and rural areas (Objectives 5b).

Soruce: Bohan, N., (1992), 'Cohesion and the Structural Funds', *The Annual Review of European Community Affairs*, (London, Brassey's, p.219.

TABLE 8:2
EC COMMISSION INITIATIVES OF COMMUNITY INTEREST

PROGRAMME	OBJECTIVE	
Rechar	Support for conversion of coal-mining areas	300m Ecu
Ecu		
Envireg	Protection of the environment in lagging regions	500m Ecu
Stride	Improve innovation and R and TD capacity of lagging regions	400m Ecu
Interreg	Prepare border regions for internal market completion.	800m Ecu
Regis	Assist integration of most remote (overseas) regions.	200m Ecu
Prisma	Improve infrastructure and business services in lagging regions.	100m Ecu
Télématique	Encourage use of advanced telecommunications in lagging regions.	200m Ecu
Leader	Foster innovatory approaches to rural development planning.	400m Ecu
Euroform	Cultivate cooperation between educational authorities leading to new qualifications.	300m Ecu
NOW	Support integration of women into the workforce.	120m Ecu
Horizon	Aid economic and social integration of handicapped people.	180m Ecu

Source: Bohan, N., (1992), 'Cohesion and the Structural Funds', *The Annual Review of European Community Affairs*, (London: Brassey's), p.222.

finances at least 20 per cent of the investment. Both principles have been invoked by regional authorities in France and elsewhere in support of their demand for a bigger say in the formulation and implementation of EU regional policy. In reality, these principles have also resulted in the channelling of increased amounts of French regional and local authority investment into EU funded projects. This pattern of functional devolution is, of course, consistent with the long-term pattern of French regionalization.

The procedures established by the Commission for the allocation of the structural funds required member-states to submit development plans corresponding to each of the EU funding priorities. As Doutriaux [*1991: 91*] has argued, the regionalized planning mechanisms established by the *Defferre* reforms combined with the existence of the national planning agency, the DATAR, left France better placed to respond to this request than the United Kingdom. Here, the ideological opposition of the Conservative government to state planning and the non-existence of elected regional bodies has almost certainly been detrimental to British regional economic interests [*Moore, 1991*]. In France, however, there was *concertation* between the DATAR, the government and regional authorities (albeit in varying degrees of intensity) in an attempt to maximize EU support for the Xth Plan. Thus, during the spring of 1989, Jacques Chérèque, Minister for Planning, personally lobbied both Jacques Delors, EU Commission President, and Bruce Millan, EU Commissioner for regional policy, following the Commission's initial response to French applications for regional assistance. His efforts were rewarded when the Commission agreed to provide additional support under Objective 1 for Corsica and the DOM-TOM as well as increased funding under Objective 5 for rural development in France (*Le Figaro*, 10 March 1989; *Le Monde*, 18 July 1989). Moreover, as Drevet [*1993*] points out, the 1982 decentralization reforms also permitted regional and local authorities to enter into transfrontier cooperation agreements, a factor which enabled French regions to benefit from EU programmes such as INTERREG.

The EU structural funds remain small and as a relatively wealthy, northern European state, France is not a major beneficiary of them. Even so, between 1989 and 1993, France received a total of FF40,000 million from EU structural funds. During the same period, the contribution of the French state to state-region *contrats de Plan* was FF52,000 million. In 1990, ERDF grants alone totalled FF3,000 million, more than the budget of the DATAR. In geographical terms, the principal beneficiaries of EU structural funds during this period were Corsica and the overseas Departments (which received 15.5 per cent), declining industrial areas (17 regions in metropolitan France were assisted) which were awarded 21.5 per cent, and rural areas (17 regions in metropolitan France were assisted), which received 36.9 per cent of EU structural funds allocated to France between 1989-93 [*Drevet, 1993: 94*]. Thus, not surprisingly, the existence of the funds has acted as a powerful magnet, attracting French regional authorities (generally keen to demonstrate their political authority) to Brussels in the hope of securing additional funding for regional development projects.

Officially responsible for the preparation of regional plans and signatories to planning contracts negotiated with the state, French regions have increasingly been drawn into the EU regional policy process, which has become linked to the national planning process. The Nord-Pas-de-Calais regional authority, for instance, was centrally involved in the negotiation and implementation of the Community Support Framework programme (Objective 2) for the region, which formed the basis of the region's planning contract for the period of the Xth Plan. The total cost of the programme for the period 1989-1991 was 724 million ECU. EU support from the CSF totalled 201 million ECU, in addition to which the region also received grants from the RECHAR and INTERREG programmes and loans from the European Investment Bank and European Coal and Steel Community [*Doutriaux, 1991: 122*].

THE REPRESENTATION OF FRENCH REGIONAL INTERESTS AT THE EU LEVEL

Formal Representation of French Regions in the EU Policy-Making Process

As highlighted above, French regional authorities have to varying degrees become increasingly affected by, and increasingly involved in, the formulation and implementation of EU policies. However, France remains a centralized, unitary state and national governments have jealously guarded their constitutional rights with regard to EU policy-making. In contrast to the German Länder and Belgian regional authorities, French regions play no formal role at the national level in the formulation of EU policy. French EU policy is the product of inter-ministerial negotiations between the DATAR and key ministries such as Industry, Employment, Agriculture, Finance and the Ministry of the Interior. Overall responsibility for coordination of EU policy lies with the *Secrétariat Général du Comité Inter-ministériel* (SGCI) for Foreign Affairs, headed by the Prime Minister [*Engel, 1992; Balme, 1992*]. Even with regard to the preparation of regional development plans, the role of the regional council and regional socio-economic interests is purely consultative. In accordance with the 1992 administrative reform it is the regional prefect who is ultimately responsible for the preparation of the regional plan and the submission of applications for EU structural fund support to the government (via the DATAR) and the EU. EU structural funds are then transmitted to regional and local authorities via the appropriate Ministries (Social Affairs for the European Social Fund, Interior for ERDF grants) [*Charpentier, 1992; Plainfosse, 1993*]. In order to be effective EU lobbyists, regional *notables* must secure the assistance and support of national politico-administrative elites involved in the formulation of EU policy. Thus, European integration has in many respects increased the need for *concertation* between regions and the state. In reality, this is often achieved through the longstanding and widespread mechanism of *cumul des mandats* which provides many local and regional politicians with direct access to government ministers.

Before the adoption of the Maastricht Treaty in 1992, French regions were formally represented at the EU level only within the European Commission. Indeed, with the exception of the German Länder who (by virtue of their federal status) have since 1987 participated in European Commission and European Council working groups and who (like Belgian regional authorities) send representatives to those Council of Ministers meetings relating to matters of their exclusive competence, this situation applied to all regional authorities. Informally, however, regional interests are represented within the European Parliament and also in the Council of Ministers by national government ministers and COREPER officials. The

French Permanent Representation, for example, usually includes a *sous-préfet*, responsible for the representation of local interests. The European Parliament provides an important forum for the representation of regional interests and has consistently campaigned for the formal representation of regions within the assembly. In 1988, the Parliament adopted a *Community Charter on Regionalization* advocating the statutory representation of regions within the Community. There is also a Parliamentary Intergroup of MEPs holding local and regional elective mandates. Within the European Commission, regional interests are represented in the Committee for the Development and Reconversion of Regions, established in 1989. This comprises national officials (and regional officials from Germany and Belgium) who are consulted over EU regional policy. In addition, the Commission, in 1988, created a Consultative Council of Regional and Local Authorities. This comprises 42 members nominated by three regional associations: the International Union of Local Authorities (IULA), the European Assembly of the Regions (ARE) and the Council of European Municipalities and Regions (CEMR).

Largely as a result of pressure from the German Länder and Belgian regions for stronger regional representation at the EU level, the Maastricht Treaty replaced the Consultative Council with a larger Committee of the Regions. The Comittee of the Regions comprises 189 local and regional authority representatives.[5] It is a consultative body, whose views must be sought on matters relating to education, culture, public health, trans-European transport networks and social cohesion. It is, of course, too early to evaluate the likely significance of the Committee. However, regional authorities throughout the EU have already voiced concern over the fact that representatives will be nominated by central governments and need not hold a local or regional authority elective mandate. French regional authorities have also expressed opposition to the inclusion of local (as opposed to regional) representatives. As Van Ginderachter [*1993*] argues, the significance of the Committee will to a considerable extent depend upon the assertiveness of its members and the scope of its activity. In addition to the Committee of the Regions, the Maastricht Treaty also extended to all regional governments the right to participate and vote (on behalf of the member-state) in Council of Ministers meetings where issues of regional competence are under discussion. In such cases, the national government Minister is to be accompanied by a single regional representative. The Maastricht Treaty has thus marginally increased the representation of regional interests at the EU level, though these provisions fell short of German and Belgian demands.

Since the mid-1980s, there has been a sharp increase in the EU lobbying activities of French regional and local authorities, which have also campaigned for the formal representation of regional interests at the EU level. Increasingly, French regional authorities have become a conduit for the representation of local socio-economic interests in Brussels [*Chauvet: 1989*]. The proliferation of interregional (and intermunicipal) cooperation reflects growing recognition on the part of the EU Commission, the state and regional authorities of the need for larger regional planning and administrative units within the context of the SEM. For French regional authorities, a high profile presence in Brussels is enormously helpful in the search for potential partners (for EU funding applications) in other EU countries. Several regional *notables* such as Charles Millon (UDF), President of the Rhônes-Alpes region and Jacques Blanc (UDF), President of Languedoc-Roussillon region, have also viewed interregional cooperation as a means of extending their own political power base. National borders have thus been transcended with the creation of 'Euro-regions', Euro-districts, Euro-cities and European regional associations whose members are geographically dispersed, but which have similar socio-economic problems and a common interest in lobbying the EU. These developments have often been encouraged and facilitated by the European Comission's attempts to develop a more coherent European regional policy. The Association of European Regions (ARE) set up in 1985 to strengthen the political representation of regions within the European Union and the Council of Europe has also played an important role raising the profile of regional and local authorities in Europe. The Europeanization of French regional government thus constitutes part of a general European trend.

There is a considerable French regional lobby in Brussels. Seventeen of the 22 French metropolitan regional authorities enjoy permanent representation there. Nord-Pas-de-Calais region opened a Brussels office in September 1989, followed by the Rhône-Alpes in Spring 1990. Brittany and Pays-de-la-Loire maintain a joint Brussels delegation. Other French regions are represented at the EU level by the Brussels offices of the two French regional federations, the *Grand Sud* and the *Grand Est*, which opened offices in Brussels in 1986 and 1989 respectively. The former comprises the regions of Aquitaine, Corsica, Languedoc-Roussillon, Midi-Pyrénées and Provence-Alpes-Côtes-d'Azur. The latter is composed of Alsace, Bourgogne, Champagne-Ardenne, Franche-Comté and Lorraine. The primary role of both federations is to facilitate integrated infrastructure planning and economic development. Picardy regional council has recently opened a Brussels office which it shares with Essex County Council from England. The overseas regional councils of Martinique and Réunion each maintains a delegation in Brussels [*Luchaire, 1990; Le Monde*, April 1992]. In addition to the regional authorities themselves, there are a number of other French 'regional' lobbyists with offices in Brussels including the

DATAR, *Breizh Europe* (an EU lobby set up by Breton SMEs) and the Nord-Pas-de-Calais regional chamber of commerce and industry [*Raux, 1991*]. The proliferation of non-governmental 'regional' lobbies in France and elsewhere has given rise to a number of disputes regarding the composition of the 'regional interest' [*Mazey and Mitchell: 1993*]. The importance of the Euro-expert or Euro-officer has been increased by the recent reforms of the EU structural funds. These are now allocated to programmes comprising multiple projects and involve other authorities within the same country or even in different member states. A primary role of the Euro-officer, therefore, is to negotiate partnerships not only with the Commission, but also with other EU regional authorities.

Though French regional politicians have expressed opposition to suggestions that the number of French regions should be reduced, they have generally supported the principle of voluntary interregional cooperation. A survey of regional politicians undertaken by *Le Monde* in 1991 revealed widespread support for this. As Jean Raffarin (UDF, Poitou-Charentes) remarked after the National Assembly debate on the 1991 Joxe local administrative reform bill, 'the region is neither a territory nor a market, but a network of mutual help procedures oriented to the exterior. Interregional cooperation is necessary for the credibility of the regional institution. Let's go forward: yes to future interregional *contrats de Plan* (*Le Monde*, 14 April 1991). Border regions, in particular, have been keen to exploit the provision under Article 65 of the 1982 reforms permitting cross-border economic cooperation.[6] This development has been further facilitated by Article 10 of the ERDF regulations which authorizes the Commission to fund transfrontier pilot projects in countries which *individually* are not eligible for assistance. This has proved to be an important incentive for French regions. Since 1986, the Rhône-Alpes regional council has signed a number of cooperation agreements in the fields of scientific and technical development with the German Land of Baden-Würtemberg, the Spanish autonomous community of Catalonia and the Italian region of Lombardy. Similarly, since 1982, a 'Euro-region' based upon the Upper Rhine area has brought together representatives of the Alsace region (France), the two Swiss cantons of Basle and the two German Länder, Baden-Würtemberg and Rhineland Palatinate, in a series of 'tripartite congresses'. These have resulted in a series of cooperation agreements covering areas such as higher education, culture, environmental protection, tourism and economic development. In 1990 this association applied for EU funding for 30 projects under the INTERREG programme, designed to prepare border regions for the internal market (*Le Monde*, 22 January 1991). The Euro-region Kent-Nord-Pas-de-Calais was set up on the initiative of the EU Commission in 1988 to promote economic cooperation between regional authorities directly affected by the channel tunnel project. In 1991, this Euro-region was extended to include Wallonia, Flanders and Brussels and now maintains its own Brussels lobby. In 1989, the Euro-region of the 'south of Europe' was set up by the three regional presidents of the Midi-Pyrénées, Languedoc-Roussillon and Catalonia. Cooperation between these regions has centred on the development of better communication links between Spain and France [*Regions of Europe, 4/1991*].

French regions are also members of the numerous regional and local associations which have proliferated since the early 1970s and which have become important EU lobbyists. These include the International Union of Local Authorities (IULA) established in 1913 and based in the Hague; the Council of European Communes (CCE) set up in 1951 and based in Paris, which became the Council of European Municipalities and Regions (CEMR) in 1984; and the Permanent Conference of Local and Regional Authorities (CPLRE) established in 1957 by the Council of Europe. Since September 1986, IULA and CEMR has jointly funded a permanent representation of regional and local authorities in Brussels. Finally, the Council of European Regions was established in 1985. Renamed the Assembly of European Regions (ARE, the acronym being based on the French version of the name *Association des Régions Européennes*) in 1987, the ARE represents 107 European regions including the Swiss cantons and Austrian Länder [*Chauvet: 1989*]. Based in Strasbourg, the principal objective of the ARE is to organize and reinforce the political representation of regions within the European Union and the Council of Europe.

The ARE in fact comprises nine interregional founding organizations, each of which continues to operate as a separate lobby within the ARE. These include: the Association of European Border Regions (AEBR); the Conference of Peripheral Maritime Regions (CRPM); the Community of the Western Alps (COTRAO); the Association of the Central Alps (ARGE-ALP); the Association of the Eastern alps (ALPEN-ADRIA); the Working Community of the Pyrenees; the Working Community of the Jura; the Community of Traditional Industrial Regions (RETI); and the Union of Regions around National Capitals. French regions are actively involved in all of these associations which have sought to promote interregional policies at the EU. The RETI, for example, which was involved in defining Objective 2 of the EU regional policy, is headed by Noël Josephe, chairperson of the Nord-Pas-de-Calais region (a major beneficiary of CSF funding under this heading).

Whilst it is relatively easy to document the above activities of French regions, it is of course much more difficult to assess the significance of these initiatives, not least because very little detailed empirical research has yet been undertaken to evaluate the policy-making impact of the 'regional' lobby in Brussels. The relatively recent arrival of many regions in Brussels means that several of them have yet to establish clear objectives and close links with policy-makers. A more general factor which further limits the effectiveness of many so-called 'regional' lobbies is their ambiguity. In reality, there is no single regional interest, but several different types of socio-economic, cultural and political interests, all of which claim in some sense to be 'regional', but which ultimately have different, sometimes conflicting policy objectives. Thus, individual regional associations and regional authorities are ultimately competing with each other for EU resources. However, given the high cost of maintaining an office in Brussels, it seems reasonable to assume that few regional authorities will stay there unless it is worth their while to do so. Moreover, it is unrealistic to attempt to measure the impact of regional authority lobbying in isolation. In reality, regions are only one of several conduits for regional interests seeking to influence EU policy outcomes. Similarly, French regional authorities rarely act alone. Typically they collaborate with other EU policy actors – notably the French state.

CONCLUSION: TOWARDS A 'EUROPE OF THE REGIONS'?

In France, as elsewhere in the EU, European integration has increased the economic and political importance of elected regional and local authorities. The Europeanization of French regional policy-making has been aided by the 1982 regional reforms which provided the institutional framework and politico-economic incentives for French regional *élus* to become involved in the EU policy process. French regional (and local) politicians are interested in the European policy process for both economic and political reasons. With the arrival of the Single European Market, regions, departments and municipalities throughout France are now anxious to describe themselves as being *'au coeur de l'Europe'*. The considerable amount of resources devoted to lobbying the EU Commission is further evidence of the importance French regional authorities attach to EU policy outcomes. Economic and financial gains are not the only consideration. The revival of the debate on a 'Europe of the Regions' reflects new hopes on the part of some regional politicians that the developments outlined above will or should lead to increased political autonomy for regions within a federal European Community [*Loughlin, 1994*]. This raises the key question of the significance of the developments outlined above for the nature of intergovernmental relations within France and the EU.

Detailed evaluation of the *economic* impact of European integration upon French regions, though clearly an important part of this debate, lies beyond the scope of this paper. The key question to be addressed here concerns the implications of European integration for French regionalization and decentralization. Essentially, two contradictory processes seem to be evident. On the one hand, the Europeanization of French regional government since 1982 represents yet a further development in the incremental development of 'functional' regional government within the framework of the nation-state. On the other hand, this has given rise to new forms of regional groupings and processes which are not linked to the nation-state and which might even come to challenge the latter's authority. These two processes are becoming increasingly difficult to reconcile within the existing legal and constitutional framework of the European Union, based as it is at present, solely upon the nation-state.

As argued above, an important consequence of the SEA and the 1992 programme has been the incorporation of French regional governments into the EU policy-making process. To the extent that this has occurred, the economic and political authority of the regions has been enhanced. Moreover, the EU lobbying activities of French regions are no longer confined to EU regional policy issues. Increasingly, they are actively engaged in lobbying the EU Commission in other policy sectors such as the environment, industrial policy and education (*Le Monde*, 20 January 1991; *Le Monde*, 21 April 1991). Yet, European integration has also imposed new constraints upon regions. The most obvious and arguably manageable limitations upon the room for manoeuvre of regional authorities derive from the primacy of EU law throughout the Union. EU competition policy, public procurement directives, environmental protection laws and the progressive harmonization of technical norms, health and safety standards, and indirect taxation throughout the EU, inevitably reduce regional autonomy. Paradoxically, however, it is national governments that remain legally responsible for ensuring the application of EU law within the member-states. This, combined with the fact that the EU may still deal formally and constitutionally only with national governments means that European integration may even centralize into a national government's hands powers which had previously been exercised by regional authorities. Bray and Morgan [*1985: 18*] explain that the process whereby 'what had previously been local government functions have to become national government functions the moment that they fall within a Community policy, since the Community cannot deal with local government or other agencies' raises the paradoxical point that a Community which in some ways seeks to challenge the authority of the nation-state in fact, in some cases, reinforce it'.

Secondly, the effective participation of French regional authorities in the EU regional policy process ultimately entails increased *concertation* with the national planning agency DATAR and the Ministry for Planning. Whilst French regions may engage in EU lobbying in an attempt to influence the nature of the regulations governing eligibility for EU structural fund support, it is the national government which presents French applications for EU funding to the EU Commission. Moreover, all applications for ERDF funding must be supported financially by the state. French regions should, therefore, bear in mind the need to lobby the national government as well as the EU Commission.

The third constraint upon the Europeanization of French regional government stems from Article 72 of the French constitution, which (since 1986) means that all activities of French regions must obtain authorization from the government. As noted by Dolez, transfrontier cooperation agreements negotiated by regions were often not transmitted to the prefect on the grounds that they were not of a commercial or industrial character. However, legislation adopted in February 1992 designed to clarify the juridical status of such agreements means that all formal agreements must now be referred to the prefect for approval [*Dolez: 1992*]. French national government spokespersons repeatedly express displeasure at what they perceive to be the foreign policy aspirations of regional governments. With regard to the planning process, for instance, government ministers and representatives of DATAR have repeatedly stressed the need for central government coordination regional initiatives (*La Croix*, 25 February 1990; *Le Monde*, 16 December 1990; *La Documentation Française, 1990*). Two prime ministerial circulars signed by Laurent Fabius in 1985 and Jacques Chirac in 1987 oblige local and regional authorities to inform the government of all formal contact with the European Commission whether this contact is made via the regional prefect or through the French Permanent Representation in Brussels. The 1987 circular indicates that whilst regional authorities may (subject to the agreement of the government) contact Commission officials for information, they may not present projects (even those relating to regional matters) to the Commission nor engage in negotiations. The official justification for this requirement is that the national government is the official partner of the EU and legally responsible for the application of EU law throughout France.

The above remarks highlight the extent to which the economic and political reality of interregional cooperation and policy-making within the EU is increasingly at odds with the legal and constitutional basis of the Union, which remains based upon the nation-state. A new complex set of relationships between the EU, national governments and regional/local authorities is evolving. As early as 1977, Hull and Rhodes [*1977*] suggested that EU membership had resulted in a shift away from 'dyadic relationships' between local authorities and the state towards 'triadic relationships' between supranational, national and sub-national governments. The completion of the SEM has accelerated this trend. As the Commission reported:

> The construction of a Europe without frontiers will strengthen relations between regions in different member-states ... Regions themselves are awakening to both the increased competition and new opportunities they face in a more integrated Europe ... There is already evidence that cities and regions are establishing new networks and other forms of cooperation to reap the benefits of economies of scale, technology transfers and increased efficiency through joint ventures (*Commission of the European Communities, 1991: 22*).

This trend was confirmed by Rhodes [*1986*] who noted that with the exceptions of Ireland (and France before 1982), EU-state-regional/local government relations had shifted away from a hierarchical model, towards a consultative model based upon formal consultation. However, he suggested the need for a third, participative model involving complex networks of intergovernmental relations (see Figure 8:1). Leonardi and Nanetti [*1990*] drew similar conclusions from their own study of the impact of the SEM on the Italian regional government of Emilia-Romagna, but went even further in emphasizing the network of horizontal relationships between regional and local authorities throughout the EU (see Figure 8:2).

As yet, however, these developments have not been legally recognized. In the absence of any such development, a major problem facing French regions seeking to establish links with regional authorities in other EU countries is the absence of an appropriate legal framework for such an association. As Anderson noted back in 1982:

> The mismatch between political and administrative organization on different sides of international boundaries creates difficulties in harmonizing practices and in setting up cooperative institutions at the local and regional levels. This problem is most acute at the frontiers of a highly centralized state such as France and a confederated state such as Switzerland [*Anderson, 1982: 15*].

Hitherto, French regions have relied upon associative structures for these purposes, but this has no standing in European or international law. This particular problems is now widely acknowledged. Meanwhile, French legislation adopted in February 1992 permits the establishment of 'Public Interest Groups' by French local authorities and those of another EU member-state 'to set up and jointly administer, for a defined period, all actions required by interregional and transfrontier cooperation programmes and projects'. A more radical solution is that proposed by the DATAR and

FIGURE 8:1
DIFFERENT FORMS OF EC-STATE-REGIONAL/LOCAL AUTHORITY
RELATIONSHIPS

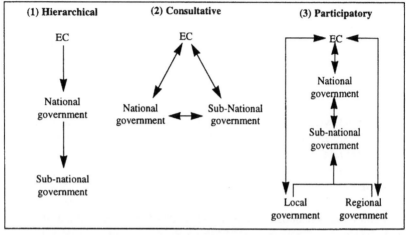

Source: Rhodes, R, *European Policy-Making, Implementation and Sub-Central Governments.*
Maastricht, European Institute of Public Administration, p.46.

FIGURE 8:2
LINKAGE NETWORKS FOR SUB-NATIONAL GOVERNMENTS AFTER THE
CREATION OF THE SINGLE MARKET

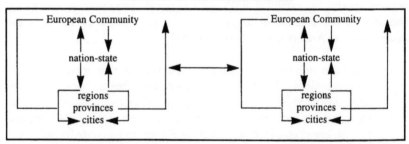

Source: Leonardi, R, and R. Nanetti, *The Regions and European Integration: The Case of Emilia-Romagna,* London, Pinter Publishers, p.11.

the *Sécrétariat Général du Comité Interministériel* that the EU create
'European governments of public interest' [*Dolez: 1992*]. Such a
development could prove to be important with regard to the future status of
transfrontier regional networks and associations. At the very least, the
current discussion on the principle of subsidiarity and the inclusion of the
principle in the Maastricht Treaty suggests that a search for some guiding
principles regarding the management of EU, national and sub-national
intergovernmental relations has finally begun within the Community.

NOTES

1. This paper forms part of a wider research project codirected by J. J. Richardson and S. Mazey on the influence of French and British interest groups on EU policy, financed by the Economic and Social Research Council (UK).
2. For a recent evaluation of the 1982 French decentralization reforms see 'L'Etat de la décentralisation', *Cahiers Français*, 256, 1992; 'La Décentralisation', *Pouvoirs*, 60, 1992.
3. In 1986, the municipalities handled 43.8 per cent of all public contracts, the departments accounted for 19.9 per cent and the regions for 3.5 per cent. (Ministère des Finances, 1989, 'Le Recensement des Marchés publics de 1986 à 1989', *Notes bleues, no. 504*).
4. At the Edinburgh European Council in December 1992, Member States agreed to increase Structural Fund expenditure to 30 billion ECU (in 1992 prices) by 1996. Of this sum, 2.6 billion ECU will be devoted the new Cohesion Fund, set up to assist the four poorest EU countries (Spain, Portugal and Ireland), meet EU environmental standards and develop trans-European transportation links.
5. Article 198A of the Maastricht Treaty states that France, Germany, Britain and Italy each have 24 representatives; Spain 21; Belgium, Greece, The Netherlands, Portugal each have 12; Denmark and Ireland each have nine and Luxembourg has six.
6. Article 65 of the 1982 decentralization reforms was clarified by prime ministerial circulars in May 1983, May 1985 and May 1987, specifying that transfrontier cooperation was to be limited to adjoining transfrontier regions, subject to government authorization and should not involve the conclusion of binding agreements. The administrative reform of 6 February 1992 permitted any local authority or group of local authorities to enter into agreements with their counterparts in neighbouring countries, but only within the limits of their competence and subject to French international agreements. All such agreements must be approved by the regional prefect.

REFERENCES

Anderson, M., 1982, 'The political problems of frontier regions', *West European Politics*, Vol.5, pp.277-318.

Auby, J-F., 1990, 'L'Europe des régions', *L'Actualité juridique – droit administratif*, 20 avril, pp.208-216.

Biancarelli, J., 1991, 'La communauté européenne et les collectivités locales: une double dialectique complexe', *Revue française d'administration publique*, No.60, octobre-décembre, pp.515-528.

Bohan, N., 1992, 'Cohesion and the structural funds', in P. Ludlow, J. Mortensen, and J. Pelkmans (eds), *The annual review of European Community Affairs 1991* (Brussels: Brassey's (UK), pp.266-275.

Bongers, P., 1990, *Local government and 1992* (Harlow: Longman).

Bray, C., and R. Morgan, 1985, *The European Community and central-local government relations: a review* (London: Economic and Social Research Council).

Cecchini, P., 1988, *The European challenge 1992: The benefits of a single market* (Aldershot: Wildwood House).

Charpentier, J., 1992, 'France', in J. Charpentier and C. Engel (eds), 1992, *Les Régions de l'Espace communautaire* (Nancy: Presses Universitaries de Nancy).

Chauvet, J-P., 1989, 'Participation des collectivités territoriales aux décisions européennes: le rôle des lobbies locaux et régionaux', *Après Demain*, No.314-315, mai-juin, pp.8-12.

Commission of the European Communities, 1990, 'The new structural policies of the European Community', *European File*, June-July.

Commission of the European Communities, 1991, *Europe 2000: outlook for the development of the Community's territory*, (Luxembourg, Office for Official Publications of the European Communities).

Dayries, J-J., and M. Dayries, 1986, *La Régionalisation* (Paris: Presses Universitaires de France).

Delcamp, A., 1993, 'La décentralisation française: a-t-elle été conçue dans une perspective européenne?, in H. Portelli (ed.), *La Décentralisation française et l'Europe* (Paris: Editions Pouvoirs Locaux), pp.57-76.

Delcamp, A., 1992, 'La décentralisation française et l'Europe', *Pouvoirs*, No.60, pp.149-160.

Deslhiat, C., 1989, 'Le Xe Plan 1989-1992', *Regards sur l'Actualité*, No.152, (Paris: La Documentation française), pp.3-35.

Dolez, B., 1992, 'Nouvelles perspectives de la coopération décentralisée', *Regards sur l'Actualité*, No.182, juin, pp.38-47.

Doutriaux, Y., 1991, *La politique régionale de la CEE* (Paris: Presses universitaires de France).

Drevet, J-F., 1993, 'La Politique régionale communautaire et la France', in H. Portelli (ed.), *La Décentralisation française et l'Europe* (Paris: Editions Pouvoirs Locaux), pp.92-96.

Duchacek, D., 1990, 'Perforated sovereignties: towards a typology of new actors in international relations', in H. J. Michelmann and P. Soldatos (eds), *Federalism and international relations: the role of sub-national units* (Oxford: Clarendon Press).

Gallacher, J., 1989, *The local economy and 1992* (Wakefield: Frontlines No.1).

Hull, C. and R. Rhodes, 1977, *Inter-governmental relations in the European Community* (Farnborough: Saxonhouse).

Keating, M and P. Hainsworth, 1986, *Decentralisation and change in contemporary France* (Aldershot: Gower).

La Documentation Française, 1990, 'Administrations et collectivités locales françaises: quel avenir dans l'Europe', *Notes et Etudes documentaires*, No.4923.

Le Monde, 1992, 'La France dans ses régions', avril.

Labasse, J., 1991, *L'Europe des Régions* (Paris: Flammarion).

Lemas, P-R., 1991, 'France', *Revue française d'administration publique*, No. 60, octobre-décembre, pp.641-646.

Leonardi, R. and R. Nanetti, 1990, *The regions and European integration: the case of Emilia-Romagna* (London: Pinter Publishers).

Loughlin, J., 1994, 'Nation, State and Region in Western Europe', in L. Beckemans (ed.), *Culture the Building-Stone of Europe 2004* (Brussels: Interuniversity Presses).

Luchaire, Y., 1990, 'Les Régions et l'Europe', *Annuaire des collectivités locales* (Paris: Librairies techniques), pp.23-35.

Mazey, S., 1987, 'Decentralization: la grande affaire du septennat?', in S. Mazey and M. Newman (eds), *Mitterrand's France* (London: Croom Helm).

Mazey, S., 1993, 'Developments at the French meso level', in L. J. Sharpe (ed.), *The rise of meso government in Europe* (London: Sage), pp.60-89.

Mazey, S., and J. Mitchell, 1993, 'Territorial interests and European integration: the Scottish experience', in S. Mazey and J. J. Richardson (eds), *Lobbying in the European Community* (Oxford: Oxford University Press).

Mény, Y., 1983, *Centres et périphéries: le partage de pouvoir* (Paris: Economica).

Moore, C., 1991, 'Regional government in the UK: proposals and prospects', *Regional Politics and Policy*, Vol.1(3), pp.223-241.

Perrin, B., 1990, 'Ententes interrégionales: des régions pour l'Europe', *Regards sur l'Actualité*, No. 164, September-October, pp.39-53.

Plainfossé, S., 1993, 'Les structures et les procédures communautaires d'aides aux collectivités locales', in H. Portelli (ed.), *La Décentralisation française et l'Europe* (Paris: Editions Pouvoirs Locaux), pp.77-91

Raux, J., 1991, 'Les implications de l'Acte unique européen pour les collectivités régionales et locales avec la CEE' in Ministère de l'Intérieur, *Les nouvelles relations Etat: Collectivités locales* (Paris: La Documentation française), pp.333-348.

Rémond, B., and J. Blanc, 1989, *Les collectivités locales* (Paris: Dalloz).

Rhodes, R., 1986, *European policy-making, implementation and subcentral governments: a survey* (Maastricht: European Institute of Public Administration).

Ricq, C., 1991, 'Les institutions interrégionales transfrontialières en Europe', in Ministère de l'Intérieur, *Les nouvelles relations Etat: Collectivités locales* (Paris: La Documentation française), pp.292-306.

Shackleton, M. 1990, *Financing the European Community* (London: Pinter).

Sharpe, L. J., (ed.), 1993, *The Rise of Meso Government in Europe* (London: Sage Publishers).

Sharpe, L. J. (ed.), 1979, *Decentralist Trends in Western Europe* (London: Sage publishers).

Van Ginderachter, J., 'La Stratégie régionale de la Communauté européen de 1986 au Traité de Maastricht de 1992' in H. Portelli (ed.), 1993, *La Decentralisation française et l'Europe* (Paris: éditions Pouvoirs Locaux), pp. 141–53.

Wright, V., 1979, 'Regionalization under the French Fifth Republic: the triumph of the functionalist approach', in L. J. Sharpe (ed.), *Decentralist Trends in Western Democracies* (London: Sage).

Notes on Contributors

Richard Balme is Research Fellow at the Fondation Nationale des Sciences Politiques, Institut d'Etudes Politiques de Bordeaux and Centre d'Etude et de Recherche sur la Vie Locale. He was Visiting Scholar at the University of Chicago in 1987 and 1988. He teaches political sociology at the IEP of Bordeaux and has research interests in the fields of urban and regional government, public policy and the organization of interests. He is co-author of *Le Territoire pour Politiques: variations européennes* (Paris: L'Harmattan, forthcoming).

Maryvonne Bodiguel is Director of Research, Centre National de la Recherche Scientifique (CNRS), at the University of Rennes I. Her specialities are environmental policy and rural sociology. Her current research includes the coordination of an international research programme on European Environmental Policy Integration. Recent publications include *Produire et Preserver l'Environnement* (Paris: L'Harmattan, 1990).

Laurence Bonnet is a PhD student at the IEP Bordeaux and is completing a thesis on a comparison of expertise in urban policy in the UK and France using Birmingham and Bordeaux as case-studies.

Henry Buller is Lecturer in Geography at the University of Paris 7. He specializes in comparative environmental politics within the European Union and European rural development. Current work includes European environmental policy integration and residential migration. Recent publications include *International Counterurbanisation* with K. Hoggart (Avebury, 1994).

Jean-Claude Douence is Professor of Public Law and first Vice-President of the University of Pau and the Pays de l'Adour. He is also Director of the Centre d'Etude des Collectivités Locales. His current research activity is into new juridical forms of public management at the local level. Recent publications include *La Commune* (Dalloz, 1994).

Elisabeth Dupoirier is Director of Research at the Fondation Nationale des Sciences Politiques in Paris. She is Director of the Observatoire Interrégional du Politique. Her main research interests are political behaviour, regional identity and public opinion studies.

Patrick Le Galès is Chargé de Recherche with the CNRS in the Centre de Recherches Administratives et Politiques in Rennes. He teaches at the Institut d'Etudes Politiques at the University of Rennes 1. Among his recent publications is *Politique urbaine et développement local, une comparaison franco-britannique* (L'Harmattan, 1993).

Guy Gilbert is Professor of Economics at the University of Nanterre-Paris X and Director of the Groupe de Recherches sur l'Administration Locale en Europe (GRALE). Among his recent publications are (with Alain Guengant) *La Fiscalité Locale en Question* (Paris: Montchrestien, 1991).

Helen Hintjens is Lecturer in Development Studies at the Centre for Development Studies, University of Wales College of Swansea. Her research interests include French overseas departments in the Caribbean and the Indian Ocean, decolonization patterns in small islands and immigaration in the UK and France. She is author of *Alternatives to Independence* (Dartmouth, 1995).

John Loughlin is Professor of European Politics at the University of Wales College of Cardiff. He is joint editor of *Regional Politics and Policy: An International Journal*. His principal research interests are comparative regional government, regionalism and federalism, and administrative reform. Recently he edited *Southern Europe Studies Guide* (London: Bowker Saur, 1993) and co-edited *La Europa de las Regiones: Una Perspectiva Intergubernamental* (University of Granada, 1994).

Sonia Mazey is Lecturer in Politics at Cambridge University and Fellow of Churchill College, Cambridge. Her research focuses upon the politics, administration and policy-making processes of France and the European Union. Recently she co-edited (with J. Richardson) *Lobbying in the European Community* (Oxford University Press, 1993) and (with Carolyn Rhodes) *The State of the European Union, vol. 3*, (Boulder: Lynne Reinner, 1995).

Claude Olivesi is Lecturer in Political Science and Director of Research at the University of Corsica in Corte. He is also a member of the Centre for Legal and Political Analysis in the same institution. He is Director of Studies in the Institut Régional d'Administration in Bastia and Chief Editor of *La Revue de Science Administrative de la Méditerranée Occidentale*. His most recent publication is a special issue of this journal on 'Les Régions à Forte Identité et le Référendum Européen'.